PROLOG MINIMANUAL

to Accompany Appleby:
Programming Languages:
Paradigm and Practice

Also available from McGraw-Hill

SCHAUM'S OUTLINE SERIES IN COMPUTERS

Most outlines include basic theory, definitions, and hundreds of solved problems and supplementary problems with answers. Titles on the current list include:

Advanced Structured Cobol
Boolean Algebra
Computer Graphics
Computer Science
Computers and Business
Computers and Programming
Data Processing
Data Structures
Digital Principles, 2d edition
Discrete Mathematics
Essential Computer Mathematics
Linear Algebra, 2d edition
Mathematical Handbook of Formulas & Tables
Matrix Operations
Microprocessor Fundamentals, 2d edition
Programming with Advanced Structured Cobol
Programming with Assembly Language
Programming with Basic, 2d edition
Programming with C
Programming with Fortran
Programming with Pascal
Programming with Structured Cobol

SCHAUM'S SOLVED PROBLEMS BOOKS

Each title in this series is a complete and expert source of solved problems containing thousands of problems with worked out solutions. Related titles on the current list include:

3000 Solved Problems in Calculus
2500 Solved Problems in Differential Equations
2000 Solved Problems in Discrete Mathematics
3000 Solved Problems in Linear Algebra
2000 Solved Problems in Numerical Analysis

Available at your College Bookstore. A complete listing of Schaum titles may be obtained by writing to: Schaum Division
McGraw-Hill, Inc.
Princeton Road, S-1
Hightstown, NJ 08520

PROLOG MINIMANUAL

to Accompany Appleby:
Programming Languages:
Paradigm and Practice

Tom Hankins
University of West Virginia
College of Graduate Studies

Thom Luce
Ohio University

McGraw-Hill, Inc.
New York St. Louis San Francisco Auckland Bogotá Caracas Hamburg
Lisbon London Madrid Mexico Milan Montreal New Delhi Paris
San Juan São Paulo Singapore Sydney Tokyo Toronto

PROLOG MiniManual to Accompany Appleby: Programming Languages:
Paradigm and Practice

Copyright © 1991 by McGraw-Hill, Inc. All rights reserved. Printed in the United States of America. Except as permitted under the United States Copyright Act of 1976, no part of this publication may be reproduced or distributed in any form or by any means, or stored in a data base or retrieval system, without the prior written permission of the publisher.

1 2 3 4 5 6 7 8 9 0 DOC DOC 9 0 9 8 7 6 5 4 3 2 1

ISBN 0-07-002579-7

This book was designed and electronically typeset in Palatino
and Univers by Professional Book Center.
The editor was Eric M. Munson;
the production supervisor was Annette Mayeski.
Cover design was done by Terry Earlywine;
copyediting was done by David Rich.
The index was prepared by Savage Indexing Services.
Project supervision was done by Business Media Resources.
R. R. Donnelley & Sons Company was printer and binder.

Trademarked products cited:
Arity and Arity/Prolog are registered trademarks of Arity Corporation.

CONTENTS

PREFACE   ix

1   A FIRST LOOK AT PROLOG   1
   1.1   BRIEF BACKGROUND   1
   1.2   ARITY PROLOG   2
   1.3   A PROLOG PROGRAM   2
        PROLOG Syntax   3
        PROLOG Terms   3
   1.4   PUTTING PROLOG TO WORK BY QUERYING THE DATABASE   4
        PROLOG Variables   5
        Variables in Facts   8

2   RULES, STRUCTURED DATA, AND THE SCOPE OF VARIABLES   9
   2.1   RULES AND HOW THEY WORK   9
        Compound Rules   10
        Complex Rules   11
   2.2   STRUCTURES   13
   2.3   THE SCOPE OF PROLOG VARIABLES   16

3   OPERATORS AND FUNCTIONS   17
   3.1   OPERATORS   17
        Comparison Operators   18
        Arithmetic Operators   18
   3.2   ARITHMETIC   20
        Math Functions   21
   3.3   USING THE OPERATORS   22

4   RECURSION AND RECURSIVE RULES   25
   4.1   RECURSION AS A GENERALIZATION OF NON-RECURSIVE RULES   26
        Stream Networks   29
   4.2   SUGGESTIONS FOR WRITING RECURSIVE RULE SETS   29

CONTENTS

- 4.3 FINDING FACTORIAL VALUES 30
- 4.4 THE TOWERS OF HANOI 32

5 LISTS 35
- 5.1 REFERENCING LISTS 35
- 5.2 EXAMINING THE ELEMENTS OF A LIST 38
  - *The Member Predicate* 38
  - *Finding Elements in Specific Positions in a List* 40
  - *Counting List Elements* 41
  - *Summing a List* 42
- 5.3 FORMING NEW LISTS 42
  - *The Append Predicate* 42
- 5.4 OTHER LIST PREDICATES 44
  - *Recognizing a List* 44
  - *The Univ Predicate* 44

6 INPUT AND OUTPUT 47
- 6.1 READING AND WRITING 51
- 6.2 DATABASE MANIPULATION PREDICATES 53
- 6.3 INPUT AND OUTPUT EXAMPLES 54
  - *Forming a List From Information in a Database* 54
  - *Printing a List* 55
  - *Creating a Menu* 55
  - *Reading Sentences* 56
- 6.4 FILE I/O 57
  - *A File I/O Example* 59

7 PROGRAM CONTROL AND PROGRAM DESIGN 61
- 7.1 CONTROLLING PROGRAM EXECUTION 61
  - *Clause Arrangement* 61
  - *Using the Cut (!) to Control Program Execution* 63
  - *A Tail-Recursive Factorial Predicate* 66
  - *Caution in Using the Cut* 66
- 7.2 PROGRAMMING SUGGESTIONS 67
  - *Planning a Program* 67
  - *Writing Code* 67

8 DEVELOPING AND DEBUGGING PROGRAMS 69
- 8.1 MODULAR DEVELOPMENT 69
- 8.2 SOME COMMON ERRORS 71
- 8.3 PROLOG'S DEBUGGING PREDICATES 72

9 A FEW ARITY PROLOG EXTRAS 77

9.1　WINDOWS　77
9.2　MOUSE RELATED THINGS　81
9.3　DATABASE MANAGEMENT　81
9.4　MENUS　83
9.5　AN EXAMPLE　87

INDEX 97

PREFACE

This MiniManual is part of a series accompanying Doris Appleby's *Programming Languages: Paradigm and Practice* (McGraw-Hill, 1991). Each mini-manual introduces the reader to one programming language. Because it has been designed to accompany Appleby's text, this manual contains only the barest background information about PROLOG and logic programming in general. Readers are referred to Chapter 6: "Logic Programming" in *Programming Languages*.

This manual is also appropriate as an auxiliary text in artificial intelligence or expert systems classes in which some or all students may want an introduction to PROLOG. Similarly, persons studying PROLOG on their own would find this manual a good place to begin.

There are several good PROLOG interpreters available today. We have chosen to use Arity Prolog for the programs in the manual because it is widely available at educational discounts and offers many extensions that are helpful for developing actual applications programs. All of the program listings in the text have been run with the Arity interpreter and, except for possible errors introduced while transferring the listings into this manuscript, will run in the form in which they are presented.

Tom Hankins
Thom Luce

PROLOG MINIMANUAL

to Accompany Appleby: Programming Languages: Paradigm and Practice

1
A FIRST LOOK AT PROLOG

PROLOG is easy to learn and fun to use. This chapter introduces the language, and begins with some comments about its development (for those who are using this mini-manual independently of Appleby's text). A look at a simple PROLOG program follows, while later sections discuss syntax and ways of getting information from a PROLOG program.

1.1 BRIEF BACKGROUND

The word PROLOG is from the phrase *"programming in logic."* Alain Colmeraurer first developed the language in France in 1970 to use in natural language parsing. David H. D. Warren and others at the University of Edinburgh constructed a PROLOG compiler called PROLOG-10 later in the 1970s. In 1981, William Clocksin and Christopher Mellish, of the Department of Artificial Intelligence of the University of Edinburgh, published *Programming in PROLOG*.[1] The book quickly became the *de facto* standard for the language. Today the terms *Edinburgh* PROLOG, *Clocksin and Mellish* (or C&M) PROLOG, *standard* PROLOG, and *classic* PROLOG all refer to PROLOG as described in that book.

PROLOG might have remained one of the many obscure languages if the Japanese had not announced in 1981 that logic programming would play a major role in the development of their fifth-generation computer. PROLOG has since flourished with the arrival of many new texts, interpreters, and compilers including those oriented to microcomputer use. PROLOG and LISP are now the two main languages for developing artificial intelligence applications.

---

[1] Clocksin, W. F. and Mellish, C. S., 1981. *Programming in PROLOG*. Berlin: Springer-Verlag.

The original PROLOG compiler was written in FORTRAN. However, most subsequent PROLOG systems have been written in C on UNIX systems, which is why many predefined PROLOG terms resemble UNIX commands.

There are several characteristics that differentiate PROLOG from other languages, especially procedural languages:

- PROLOG does not distinguish between program code and program data.
- PROLOG systems use few, if any, reserved words.
- PROLOG does not execute code sequentially.
- PROLOG allows the user to define new operators with a single line of code.
- PROLOG is a conversational language, i.e., it allows the user to carry on a kind of conversation with the computer.

1.2 ARITY PROLOG

There are many implementations of PROLOG available. One of the best is Arity Prolog from Arity Corporation. This is the version we will use for all of the examples in this text.

1.3 A PROLOG PROGRAM

A PROLOG program is often called a *database* or, sometimes, simply a *base*. It is appropriate to think of a PROLOG program as a database because it contains lists of facts and rules about objects and relationships among those objects. Rather than a list of instructions, as in a procedural language program, the PROLOG program is a collection of information describing a particular situation.

Three types of statements may be used in a PROLOG program. One type declares *facts* about objects and their relationships. A second type defines *rules* about objects and their relationships. The third type asks *questions* about the objects and their relationships. As you can see, PROLOG is well suited to problems that can be expressed in the form of objects and their relationships. The objective of the programmer is to provide information about the *limited world* on which the PROLOG system will operate.

PROLOG is not so well suited to some other types of tasks. You will see later that procedural tasks such as input and output, arithmetic, and matrix manipulation, can be performed in PROLOG, but they are often awkward.

The PROLOG term for a statement in a database is *clause*. First, we will consider programs consisting of clauses that represent facts but not rules; Listing 1.1 is such a program. In it, the clauses describe kinship relations in a family. These familiar relations lend themselves to illustrating many characteristics of a PROLOG database; therefore, you will see this example expanded in later chapters.

PROLOG Syntax

Syntax refers to rules for writing clauses. The rules in PROLOG are rigid, but they are also very simple and easy to learn. The general form of the statements in the Listing 1.1 is:

```
relationship(person_1, person_2).
```

The relationship is written first and always begins with a lower-case letter. The names of the persons who are related are enclosed in parentheses and separated by a comma. The statement ends with a period. The names of the related persons also begin with lower-case letters; this indicates that the persons are specific individuals, constant values which will not change. Whenever multiword names are necessary, underscores connect the words.

Read the facts in Listing 1.1 with the first person having the indicated relationship with the second person. For example, read `mother_of(edith, dick)` so that its English equivalent is: "Edith is the mother of Dick." The other relations in the program follow the same structure. If you preferred, you could reverse the persons to `mother_of(dick, edith)`. The new statement would translate to "The mother of Dick is Edith." Either way is acceptable and will work fine as long as you are consistent and do not mix the two in a program.

You can insert comments into a PROLOG program by enclosing them with a beginning /* and an ending */. The first line of Listing 1.1 is a comment. Another way to add a comment is to precede it with the percent sign (%). Any text on a line following the % is interpreted as a comment. Note that if you comment with the %, you must repeat it on each line.

PROLOG Terms

Facts are the simplest kind of PROLOG statement. To this point, the examples have illustrated facts which describe a relationship *among* objects. However, a fact can also describe the character or condition of a single object. For example, the family database might well include facts describing gender:

```
male(luke).
female(sarah).
```

It is easy to think of many other examples such as `tall(kareem)`, `dirty(my_car)`, and `lovely(meryl)`.

The words indicating the relationships in facts are also known as *predicates*. The terms enclosed in parentheses are called *arguments* to the predicate. The number of arguments that a predicate has is the *arity*[2] of the predicate.

If a predicate appears in a program with different numbers of arguments, PROLOG will recognize the two as separate relationships. Thus, it is perfectly fine to include both of these facts in a database:

```
shoe(loafer).             /*  shoe/1  */
shoe(trigger,wednesday).  /*  shoe/2  */
```

The first fact could report that a loafer is a kind of shoe while the other might say that Trigger is to be shod on Wednesday. The comments following the predicates show the customary way of indicating a predicate and its arity. We will use this predicate-name/arity notation throughout the text.

Predicates can have any number of arguments, as these examples with arity of 3, 4, and 7 respectively indicate:

```
weather(new_orleans, summer, hot).
president(lincoln, kentucky, 1861, 1865).
class(is590, PROLOG, thursday, 6, 9, sullivan_hall, 511).
```

1.4 PUTTING PROLOG TO WORK BY QUERYING THE DATABASE

You retrieve information from a PROLOG database by asking questions, often called *goals*. A goal is attained (or, as PROLOG programmers say, it *succeeds*) if there are facts that *match*[3] or *unify*[4] the clauses in the goal. A clause and a fact unify if

1. their predicates are the same,
2. their arity is the same, and
3. their corresponding arguments are identical.

If there is no match for the clauses in a goal, the goal *fails*.

The simplest queries are ones that require a yes or no answer. Using the family database of Listing 1.1 we can ask questions, and PROLOG will respond. The first two questions in Figure 1.1 are of this type. To answer them, PROLOG searches the database for a fact that matches the goal. If it finds a match, it responds with "yes"; if it does not find a match, it answers "no."

---

[2] Not to be confused with Arity Prolog.
[3] Used here with its common meaning.
[4] Used interchangeably with *match* throughout this text. Every PROLOG system has a unification algorithm that defines in detail the way in which elements unify.

1.4 PUTTING PROLOG TO WORK BY QUERYING THE DATABASE

```
/* General form:  relationship(person1, person2).  */

        mother_of(edith, dick).
        mother_of(edith, tom).
        mother_of(sadie, calvin).
        mother_of(sadie, alice).
        mother_of(sadie, floyd).
        mother_of(gertie, john_benford).
        mother_of(gertie, edith).
        mother_of(gertie, vivian).
        mother_of(jane, luke).
        mother_of(jane, sarah).
        mother_of(jane, rachel).
        mother_of(marcy, heidi).
        mother_of(marcy, gretchen).
        mother_of(linda, andrew).

        step_father_of(tom, heidi).
        step_father_of(tom, gretchen).

        father_of(floyd, tom).
        father_of(floyd, dick).
        father_of(john_h, floyd).
        father_of(john_h, calvin).
        father_of(john_h, alice).
        father_of(john_r, vivian).
        father_of(john_r, edith).
        father_of(john_r, john_benford).
        father_of(john_benford, terri).
        father_of(tom, luke).
        father_of(tom, sarah).
        father_of(tom, rachel).
        father_of(tom, andrew).
```

LISTING 1.1 Family relationship database

PROLOG Variables

You can ask more useful questions of PROLOG by placing *variables* in your queries.[5] PROLOG variables function as place holders in an argument list, and they always begin with an upper-case letter. For example, Child is a variable in the relationship `mother_of(gertie, Child)`; it represents no specific person, but in a search, PROLOG will match `mother_of(gertie, Child)` with all three of these facts in Listing 1.1:

```
        mother_of(gertie, john_benford).
        mother_of(gertie, edith).
        mother_of(gertie, vivian).
```

---
5 Do not confuse a PROLOG variable with variables in procedural languages. PROLOG variables do *not* identify a storage location in memory.

By using variables, you can ask "who" questions of the database, as in questions 3 through 7 in Figure 1.1. Keep in mind that while PROLOG reports Jane as the only argument in the database that matches with `mother_of(X, sarah)`, it has no idea that Sarah is Jane's daughter.

Notice, too, that when there is more than one match of the variable X with an argument, PROLOG finds them all. However, after the first match is reported, you must tap the semicolon key to see the next one. When there are no more matches to report, PROLOG responds with "no."

To see how PROLOG finds its answers to these queries, consider question 4 in Figure 1.1. PROLOG reads through the database until it comes to a `father_of` relationship with `tom` as the first argument, matches the listing in the database with `father_of(tom, luke)`, and gives X the value `luke`. The PROLOG term for associating a variable with a specific constant is *instantiation*; in this case, PROLOG *instantiates* X to `luke`. It then proceeds to find `sarah`, `rachel`, and `andrew` in the same way. When it runs out of `father_of` relationships, PROLOG quits searching.

Queries 6, 7, and 11 introduce a special PROLOG variable called the *anonymous* variable, which is indicated by a single underscore. The anonymous variable matches with anything, but PROLOG does not report the matches. In the example of query 6, PROLOG reports all 14 of the first arguments in the `mother_of` relationship, regardless of the name in the second argument. Question 7 is similar except that the anonymous variable is used as the first argument.

PROLOG allows you to use the comma (,) as an *and* operator to combine clauses into compound questions. Question 8 is a query with no variables. To respond to it, PROLOG searches for a match for `father_of(john_h, floyd)` and, after finding a match, finds the match for `mother_of(sadie, floyd)` and reports "yes" to indicate its successful search.

Questions 9, 10, and 11 have *shared* variables, i.e., variables that occur in two or more goals of the query. Shared variables provide a means of constraining a request by restricting the range of the variables. For example, question 9 asks PROLOG to return only persons who are children of both John R and Gertie, and question 10 asks for any persons who are children of Marcy and Tom.

Query 11 introduces another PROLOG operator. PROLOG reads the vertical bar (|) and the semicolon (;) as a logical *or*. This goal asks for the names of persons in the database who are Gertie's children and who also are either a mother *or* a father. Notice the parentheses, which are necessary to identify the OR[ed] items.

1.4 PUTTING PROLOG TO WORK BY QUERYING THE DATABASE

PROLOG QUERY AND RESPONSE   **AN ENGLISH EQUIVALENT**

1. `father_of(john_r, vivian).`
   `yes`
   Is John R. the father of Vivian?

2. `mother_of(jane, gretchen).`
   `no`
   Is Jane the mother of Gretchen?

3. `mother_of(X, sarah).`
   `X = jane ->;`
   `no`
   Who is the mother of Sarah?

4. `father_of(tom, X).`
   `X = luke ->;`
   `X = sarah ->;`
   `X = rachel ->;`
   `X = andrew ->;`
   `no`
   Who are Tom's children?

5. `father_of(X, gretchen).`
   `no`
   Who is the father of Gretchen?

6. `mother_of(X, _).`
   `X = edith ->;`
   `. . .`
   `X = linda ->;`
   `no`
   Who is a mother?

7. `step_father_of(_, X).`
   `X = heidi ->;`
   `X = gretchen ->;`
   `no`
   Who has a step_father?

8. `father_of(john_h, floyd),`
   `mother_of(sadie, floyd).`
   `yes`
   Are John H. and Sadie the parents of Floyd?

9. `mother_of(gertie, X),`
   `father_of(john_r, X).`
   `X = john_benford ->;`
   `X = edith ->;`
   `X = vivian ->;`
   `no`
   Who are the children of Gertie and John R.?

10. `mother_of(marcy, X),`
    `father_of(tom, X).`
    `no`
    Do any children have Marcy and Tom as parents?

11. `mother_of(gertie, X),`
    `(mother_of(X, _) |`
    `father_of(X, _)).`
    `X = john_benford ->;`
    `X = edith ->;`
    `X = edith ->;`
    `no`
    Which of Gertie's children are parents?

FIGURE 1.1 Queries to PROLOG

In response to the query, PROLOG searches the list until it finds a mother_of(gertie...) relationship and notes the name of the child in that match (edith). It then searches for a mother_of or father_of relationship with the first argument edith. It finds two of these and so will report edith as an answer to the query twice. Failing in its search for more edith relationships, PROLOG returns to mother_of(gertie. . .) and looks for other second arguments. It finds john_benford and continues as it had for edith. After exhausting the possibilities for john_benford, PROLOG looks for other children of Gertie, and, finding none, quits the search.

Variables in Facts

Variables are also occasionally useful for stating facts in a database. As an example, times(0, X, 0) could indicate that anything times zero is zero. You could write the relationship breathes(_) to say that everyone breathes; but beware, it also will tell PROLOG that *anything* breathes.

2
RULES, STRUCTURED DATA, AND THE SCOPE OF VARIABLES

This chapter introduces two extensions to the PROLOG database. *Rules* allow PROLOG to infer new facts from existing facts. *Structures* allow PROLOG to manipulate a complex set of data as though it were a single item. The chapter concludes with an explanation of the scope of PROLOG variables.

2.1 RULES AND HOW THEY WORK

A PROLOG rule states a general relationship that may be used to conclude a specific fact. A synonym is an example of a simple rule. In English we use dad as a synonym for father and recognize that any person who is a father is a dad. To be more specific, one might say: Person A is person B's dad, if person A is the father of person B.

PROLOG is much more succinct. To define dad as a synonym for father, just write

    dad(X,Y) :- father_of(X,Y).

In this statement `dad(X,Y)` is known as the *conclusion* of the rule; it is also called the *head* of the rule. The right side, `father_of(X,Y)`, is the *requirement* or *condition* for finding a successful conclusion to the rule; this part of the rule is also referred to as the *body*. Between the head and body of the rule is the two-character symbol *:-* sometimes called the *neck*; you can read this as *if*. Note that the rule ends with a period.

A PROLOG fact is nothing more than a rule without a body. PROLOG will accept facts written as `father_of(floyd, dick) :-.`, but adding the if-operator is not necessary.

Another example of a simple rule is the fact that a person is a parent if she is a mother. In PROLOG we could write

```
parent_of(X,Y) :- mother_of(X,Y).
```

If we add this rule to the family database of Program 1.1, we can ask who is a parent with this query

```
?- parent_of(Who,_).
```

and PROLOG will respond with

```
Who = edith ->
```

What does PROLOG do to obtain this response? It begins by finding parent_of as the head of a rule. It then examines the conditions of the rule. In this case, `mother_of` is the first and only condition, so PROLOG begins to examine that list of facts. The first one is `mother_of(edith, dick)`. PROLOG uses those two variables to instantiate the corresponding variables in the rule head: `parent_of(edith, dick)`. Our query only requested the value of the first variable, so PROLOG reports `Who = edith`. If asked for another response (which is done by pressing the semicolon key), PROLOG examines the next `mother_of` fact and repeats the process. If it finds no more `mother_of` facts to examine, it gives up the search.

Compound Rules

Compound rules are those with more than one requirement. As an example, consider a grandmother. One sufficient condition for being a grandmother is to be the mother of a child who is also a mother. We can write this in PROLOG as

```
grandmother_of(X,Z) :- mother_of(X,Y), mother_of(Y,Z).
```

If you read the comma in this statement as "and," the statement says that X is the grandmother of Z if X is the mother of Y *and* Y is the mother of Z.

If we query the database with `grandmother_of(X,Z)`, PROLOG finds the grandmother rule and looks at the first condition. Next, it goes to the list of `mother_of` facts and instantiates X and Y to the corresponding arguments of the first fact in the list, X = edith and Y = dick. Its next step is to look at the second condition. Because that condition has a Y in it, PROLOG begins again at the top of the mother_of list looking for a match for `mother_of(dick,_)`.

After finding no match for dick as the first argument of `mother_of`, PROLOG returns to the first condition and instantiates its arguments to those of the second fact in the `mother_of` list, edith and tom. It proceeds again to the second condition, this time with Y instantiated to tom. Again it finds no match for the second condition.

It is not until the first condition is instantiated to `mother_of(gertie,edith)` and the second condition becomes `mother_of(edith,_)` that PROLOG finds a match. The first one it discovers is `mother_of(edith,dick)` and then, at the next fact in the list, `mother_of(edith,tom)`. After returning

```
X = gertie
Z = dick ->;

X = gertie
Z = tom ->;
```

for the two matches, PROLOG continues its exhaustive search of the database. When it has examined all the possibilities, PROLOG quits.

Another type of compound rule is that in which only one condition *or* another, or one condition out of several, need be true for the conclusion to hold. The `parent_of` relationship illustrates this nicely. One person is the parent of another if the first person is either the mother or the father of the second person.

There are two ways to write this in PROLOG. One is to use the semicolon (;) to write

```
parent_of(X,Y) :- mother_of(X,Y) ; father_of(X,Y).
```

Alternatively, we can write

```
parent_of(X,Y) :- mother_of(X,Y).
parent_of(X,Y) :- father_of(X,Y).
```

The latter version is used most often because it is easier to read, especially if the conditions are long. It is the form used for the programs in this book.

While the semicolon is not recommended in rules, it is necessary for queries. For example, to ask about the father or step father of Heidi, you must write

```
father_of(X,heidi) ; step_father_of(X,heidi)
```

Returning to our `grandmother_of` rule, what is necessary to have it include all the possibilities for being a grandmother? The existing rule need not be changed. All that needs to be done is to add this second `grandmother_of` rule:

```
grandmother_of(X,Z) :- mother_of(X,Y), father_of(Y,Z).
```

Complex Rules

Rules are not limited to having only facts as their conditions; they also may have other rules as a part of their requirements. For example, let's make use of our `parent_of` rule in defining a grandmother. A person is a grandmother if she is the mother of a person who is the parent of someone. We can write

```
grandmother_of(X,Z) :- mother_of(X,Y),
                       parent_of(Y,Z).
```

Given this definition of `grandmother_of`, look at how PROLOG responds to the query

```
grandmother_of(Grandmother, Grandchild)
```

The first step is to find the `grandmother_of` rule and then examine its first condition, in this case, `mother_of(X,Y)`. X and Z in the rule's head are uninstantiated at this point, and so the X in `mother_of` is also uninstantiated. PROLOG goes to the `mother_of` list and begins by instantiating X to `edith` and Y to `dick`. After that, it finds the next (and last) condition in the rule, `parent_of`.

Y is now instantiated to `dick`. PROLOG looks at the *first* `parent_of` rule (remember, there are two) and finds its first and only condition is `mother_of(X,Y)`. PROLOG now searches the list of `mother_of` facts trying to find one with `dick` as the first argument.

After failing in that attempt, PROLOG examines the next `parent_of` rule. Its condition is `father_of(X,Y)` so PROLOG goes off looking for a `father_of` relationship with `dick` as the first argument.

Failing again, PROLOG returns to the `mother_of` portion of the `grandmother_of` rule and instantiates X and Y to `edith` and `tom`, respectively. This produces no success as PROLOG examines the first `parent_of` rule, but when it goes to the second one, PROLOG finds four sets of matches:

```
Grandmother = edith
Grandchild = luke ->;

Grandmother = edith
Grandchild = sarah ->;

Grandmother = edith
Grandchild = rachel ->;

Grandmother = edith
Grandchild = andrew ->;
```

Continuing in the same fashion, PROLOG finds an additional five sets of matches before it completes its exhaustive search:

```
Grandmother = sadie
Grandchild = tom ->;

Grandmother = sadie
Grandchild = dick ->;

Grandmother = gertie
Grandchild = terri ->;

Grandmother = gertie
Grandchild = dick ->;

Grandmother = gertie
Grandchild = tom ->;
```

2.2 STRUCTURES

PROLOG allows you to nest relationships. At times this is very convenient. As an example consider this long relationship:

```
class(prolog, thursday, 6, 9, jeanne, reid, sullivan, 517).
```

It defines a *class* relationship among eight separate items. Alternatively, we could give PROLOG the same information with this statement:

```
class(prolog,
      time(thursday, 6, 9),
      instructor(jeanne, reid),
      location(sullivan, 517)   ).
```

Relationships like these are called *structures*. Although they may take a little longer to type than the first version, they make it much easier for a reader to understand the meaning of the arguments. They also have a related advantage of allowing meaningful rules like these:

```
teaches(Instructor, Day) :-
                    class(Classname,
                          time(Day, Start, Finish),
                          Instructor,
                          Location ).
instructor(Instructor, Class) :-
                    class(Class,
                          Time,
                          Instructor,
                          Location   ).
```

Pay particular attention to the second of these two rules. The English word "instructor" appears there three times, once as the name of the rule and twice as a variable. The variable, Instructor, represents the same entity in both occurrences. In this case that entity is the clause `instructor(X,Y)`. *PROLOG can instantiate a variable to a clause.*

Listing 2.1 contains a list of class relationships and these two rules. Figure 2.1 presents some queries to that database and the results of the queries. The results show that PROLOG avoids confusing the *instructor rule* with the *instructor clause* used in defining *class*. However, were we to add to the database facts of the form `instructor(linda, maier)`, PROLOG would not know which instructor we meant. In response to the query `instructor(A,B)`, PROLOG would list all of the instructors and the classes they teach as listed in the *class* definitions, and it would also list all of the instructors in the list of *instructor* facts.

```
class(prolog,
      time(thursday, 6, 9),
      instructor(jeanne, reid),
      location(sullivan, 517)     ).

class(micro_applications,
      time(tuesday, 6, 9'),
      instructor(bill, kroesser),
      location(sullivan, 511)     ).

class(database,
      time(wednesday, 1, 4),
      instructor(bob, hutton),
      location(administration, 312)).

class(data_structures,
      time(monday, 6, 9),
      instructor(dave, mader),
      location(wallace, 718)      ).

class(intro,
      time(monday, 5, 6),
      instructor(linda, maier),
      location(sullivan, 529)     ).

class(project,
      time(tuesday, 5,6),
      instructor(bill, kroesser),
      location(sullivan, 301)     ).

class(pascal,
      time(thursday, 6, 9),
      instructor(polly, cushman),
      location(sullivan, 511)     ).

teaches(Instructor, Day) :-   class(Classname,
                                    time(Day, Start, Finish),
                                    Instructor,
                                    Location ).

instructor(Instructor, Class) :- class(Class,
                                       Time,
                                       Instructor,
                                       Location ).
```

LISTING 2.1 A database with structures

What instructors teach on Thursday?

```
?- teaches(Instructor, thursday).
Instructor = instructor(jeanne, reid)
Instructor = instructor(polly, cushman)
```

What classes does Bill Kroesser teach?

```
?- instructor(instructor(bill, kroesser), Class).
Class = micro_applications
Class = project
```

What days does Jeanne Reid teach?

```
?- teaches(instructor(jeanne, reid), Day).
Day = thursday
```

Who teaches the PROLOG class?

```
?- instructor(Instructor, prolog).
Instructor = instructor(jeanne, reid)
```

or

```
?- instructor(instructor(Fname,Lname),prolog).
Fname = jeanne
Lname = reid
```

Who teaches classes that run from 6 to 9 on Mondays?

```
?- class(_,time(monday, 6, 9), Instructor, _).
Instructor = instructor(dave, mader)
```

What classes are held in room 511 of Sullivan Hall?

```
?- class(Class, _, _, location(sullivan, 511)).
Class = micro_applications
Class = pascal
```

FIGURE 2.1 Some queries to Listing 2.1

Suppose you needed to ask frequent questions about the location of classes. You could avoid the need to query with the class rule and the anonymous variables it requires by adding a rule like this to the database:

```
room(Class,Building,Room) :- class(Class,
                                   Time,
                                   Teacher,
                                   location(Building,
                                            Room)     ).
```

Using this rule, you can find out the classes in room 511 of Sullivan with the query

```
room(Class,sullivan,511)
```

Similarly,

```
room(prolog,Building,Room)
```

would cause PROLOG to report the location of the PROLOG class.

Those of you who are familiar with other programming languages may recognize these nested relations as PROLOG's equivalent of records. Each relationship is a field in the record. This *structured* data type is useful in PROLOG as elsewhere because of its ability to reflect the characteristics of a situation.

2.3 THE SCOPE OF PROLOG VARIABLES

The scope of a variable is the portion of a program that can refer to the variable. While this can be complicated to define in some languages, it is simple in PROLOG. The scope of a PROLOG variable is just the fact, rule, or query that contains it.

To illustrate this, consider this rule:

```
likes(Person, shish_kebab) :-
        likes(Person, grilled_vegetables),
        likes(Person, grilled_meat).
```

The scope of the variable *Person* is the entire rule. This means that, if we give PROLOG a goal of the form

```
?- likes(john, shish_kebab).
```

then `Person` will be instantiated to *john* as PROLOG determines the answer. Similarly, in responding to the query

```
?- likes(Person, shish_kebab).
```

PROLOG will instantiate `Person` to each name it finds in the list of relationships in the database with the form `likes(Name, Something)`. In every instance, `Person` will be instantiated to one constant at a time.

If `Person` is used in other relationships in the database, those instances have no relationship to the `Person` variable in this rule.

3
OPERATORS AND FUNCTIONS

PROLOG was not designed to manipulate numbers. Nevertheless, numeric operations are a part of many PROLOG programs that are not really numeric. These are some examples:

- Incrementing and decrementing coordinates to move a chess piece
- Counting items in a list
- Sorting or otherwise comparing items by size or order

This chapter begins by explaining the use of PROLOG's two groups of operators, the comparison operators and the arithmetic operators. These are built-in PROLOG predicates, set up so that they can be used without the normal predicate syntax. Next is a short section describing the arithmetic operator, followed by one on built-in math functions. The chapter concludes with examples that use some of the operators and functions.

3.1 OPERATORS

The normal syntax for PROLOG predicates is to list the name of the predicate followed by its list of arguments in parentheses followed by a period. An example is

```
greater_than(Item1, Item2).
```

Operators that follow this syntax are called *prefix* operators. An alternative syntax is to put the predicate between the items being compared; these are *infix* operators. Substituting the symbol ">" for greater_than, we can write the above statement in infix form as

```
Item1 > Item2.
```

Because this syntax is used so often for arithmetic and comparison operations, most PROLOG systems allow its use. Remember that both forms mean the same thing to PROLOG: a data structure that can be evaluated as true or false.

Comparison Operators

Arity Prolog's comparison operators compare two terms and evaluate their alphanumeric values. The == operator determines if two terms are equivalent, and the \== operator determines if two terms are not equivalent. For example the expression cat == cat would be true and cat \== cat would be false. The relative order operators are @<, @>, @=<, and @>=. Use these to determine less-than, greater-than, less-than-or-equal-to, and greater-than-or-equal-to, relationships respectively. You can use *not* in an expression with any of these operators.

Be careful not to confuse the = unification operator with the == comparison operator. The unification predicate combines the two terms if possible. The comparison predicate determines if the two terms are equivalent but has no other effect on them. As an example, consider the following statements:

```
X = 'Zooey'.
X == 'Zooey'.
```

The first statement gives X the value Zooey, and the statement succeeds. The second case will succeed if X has already been instantiated to Zooey; otherwise, it will fail.

Arity Prolog provides a prefix operator that either tests for or returns a comparison value. The operator is *compare*, and its form is

```
compare(Relationship, Term1, Term2)
```

If Relationship is an uninstantiated variable, *compare* returns the symbol (=, > or <) which describes the relationship between Term1 and Term2. Otherwise, it returns a true or false value.

Arithmetic Operators

PROLOG implementations vary in the arithmetic operators they provide. Arity Prolog offers the usual addition (+), subtraction (-), multiplication (*), and division (/) operators. In addition it includes operators to raise a number to a power (^), a modulo operator (mod), and a predicate to round a number.

Figure 3.1 lists Arity Prolog's arithmetic operators for the common arithmetic operations and provides examples of their use. It also includes two built-in real number constants provided in Arity Prolog, pi and random. Each is replaced in the expression in which it appears by a real number; *pi* is replaced by the value of pi and *random* is replaced by a random number with a value between and 0 and 1.

3.1 OPERATORS

- `+`   Addition

    Example: `?- X is 1 + 2.`
                     `X = 3`

- `-`   Subtraction

    Example: `?- X is 2 - 1.`
                     `X = 1`

- `*`   Multiplication

    Example: `?- X is 3 * 2.`
                     `X = 6`

- `/`   Ordinary division (result is floating point)

    Example: `?- X is 7.0 / 3.`
                     `X = 2.33`

- `//`   Integer division (result is integer)

    Example: `?- X is 7 // 3.`
                     `X is 2`

- `mod`   Modulo

    Example: `?- X is 75 mod 12.`
                     `X = 3`

- `^`   Exponential

    Example   `?- X is 2 ^ 3.`
                     `X = 8`

- `round(X,N)`   returns X rounded to N decimal places; N must be an integer between 0 and 15. Use a negative number to round to whole number positions, for example: *round*(X, -1) to round to the nearest 10's positon.

    Example: `RoundedValue is round(1.234, -1).`

- `pi`   Wherever pi appears, Arity substitutes the value of pi to 15 decimal places in the expression

- `random`   Wherever random appears, Arity substitutes a random number between 0 and 1 in the expression

Note that an arithmetic expression is not evaluated until the expression appears as an argument to an arithmetic evaluable predicate.

FIGURE 3.1 The common arithmetic operators

To compare arithmetic expressions, Arity Prolog allows you to use the standard inequality operators (>, <, >=, <=). To test the equality of two arithmetic expressions use =:= and use =\= to test for their inequality.

3.2 ARITHMETIC

The word *is* tells PROLOG to perform the calculations for a following arithmetic expression. It is another of PROLOG's infix operators that does not require the normal predicate syntax. The general form for using it is

```
<variable> is <arithmetic_expression>
```

The following example illustrates its use.

```
bonus(Number) :- Number is 2 + 3.
?- bonus(3).
no
?- bonus(5).
yes
?- bonus(X).
X = 5 ->
```

PROLOG evaluates the arithmetic expression first and then does one of two things:

1. If the variable is not instantiated, PROLOG instantiates it to the value of the expression.
2. If the variable is already instantiated, PROLOG compares the variable's value and the expression's value; only if the two are the same, does the goal succeed.

PROLOG implementations traditionally provided only integer numbers, but newer ones, including Arity Prolog, can manipulate both integer and real numbers. Arity Prolog integers range from −2,147,483,648 to 2,147,438,647. Be certain to use a space to separate integers from the periods that end clauses; in some PROLOG implementations, numbers with a period are always interpreted as real.

Real numbers in Arity Prolog may range in magnitude from $-1.7e^{308}$ to $1.7e^{308}$. You may write real numbers either with exponents as in scientific notation or in the standard way with decimal points, although you must include a digit both before and after the decimal point. *Caution*: Because floating-point operations are inexact, an attempt to unify two apparently equal floating-point numbers may not succeed.

Real numbers can be used in *is* clauses.

```
Example:  X is 0.1 * Y   (as a condition in a rule)
```

Real numbers also can be used in a clause that unifies them with a variable.

Example: X = 3.14

Notice the difference in how PROLOG evaluates the following two expressions.

```
?- X is 5 + 2.           ?- X = 5 + 2.
X = 7 ->                 X = 5 + 2 ->
```

In the first example, PROLOG evaluates the arithmetic expression and unifies X with the result, 7. In the second example, PROLOG instantiates the variable X to 5 + 2.

When integers and real numbers are both in an arithmetic expression, the integers are converted to real numbers before PROLOG performs the calculation. The result is a real number. You can explicitly convert real numbers to integers with the predicate *integer(X)*. Similarly you can convert an integer to a real number with the predicate *float(X)*.

If the result of a calculation is a number that is too large or too small to be expressed, Arity Prolog returns the atom *err*.

Math Functions

The Arity Prolog math functions work with integers, real numbers, and with both types used together, but all of the functions return real numbers. PROLOG assumes that angles are measured in radians. The general syntax for all the functions is

```
X is function(Y)
```

where X is an unbound variable and Y is a bound variable or a number. Figure 3.2 lists the math functions available in Arity Prolog.

`abs()`	absolute value
`sqrt()`	square root
`exp()`	natural log base e raised to the value's power
`ln()`	natural log of the value
`log()`	decimal log of the value
`sin()`	sine
`cos()`	cosine
`tan()`	tangent
`asin()`	arc sine
`acos()`	arc cosine
`atan()`	arc tangent

FIGURE 3.2 Math functions

3.3 USING THE OPERATORS

One entry in the database of a wholesale liquor distributor contains the brand name and the proof of the liquor. These are some of the entries:

```
proof(jims_beam, 160).
proof(old_logger, 177).
proof(johnny_runner, 130).
proof(some_times, 180).
```

The company found that they sometimes needed to report the percentage of alcohol in the liquors instead of the proof. To facilitate that reporting, they added this rule to the database.

```
percent(Liquor, Percent_alcohol) :-
     proof(Liquor, Proof),
     Percent_alcohol, is Proof / 2.
```

This rule allows queries like this:

```
?- percent(old_logger, Percent_alcohol).
Percent_alcohol = 88.5
```

They can also get reports on all items by asking

```
?- percent(Liquor, Percent_alcohol).
Liquor = jims_beam
Percent = 80.0
Liquor = old_logger
Percent = 88.5
Liquor = johnny_runner
Percent = 65.0
Liquor = some_times
Percent = 90.0
```

An example in which the arithmetic is a little more complex is a database containing the average annual temperature of cities. The climatologist who first set up the database entered all of the temperatures in degrees fahrenheit. Here are some of the entries.

```
ave_temp(addis_ababa, 62).
ave_temp(berlin, 49).
ave_temp(calgary, 38).
ave_temp(belgrade, 52).
ave_temp(chicago, 50).
ave_temp(boston, 48).
ave_temp(washington_dc, 55).
ave_temp(jerusalem, 61).
ave_temp(khartoum, 84).
ave_temp(san_diego, 61).
```

These worked fine several years ago, but now she needs to use Celsius temperatures most of the time. Rather than reenter all of her data, she added this rule to her database.

```
ave_temp_celsius(Location, C_temp) :-
    ave_temp(Location, F_temp),
    C_temp is round((F_temp - 32) * 5 // 9, 0).
```

This lets her obtain the Celsius temperature with queries like this:

```
?- ave_temp_celsius(berlin, C_temp).
C_temp = 9.0
```

She can also check the database to find all locations with a particular Celsius temperature with this query:

```
?- ave_temp_celsius(Location, 16.0).
Location = jerusalem ->;
Location = san_diego ->;
```

A final example uses the greater-than comparison operator. As an exercise, a high school geography teacher requires his students to compare pairs of cities and determine from their latitudes and longitudes which of the pair is further north and which is further west. How would an enterprising student get PROLOG to figure this out?

The only problem in creating the fact base would be selecting the name for the relationship. Let's assume that it is called "location" and the order of arguments are city, latitude, and longitude. Assume also that the programmer chooses to enter south latitudes and east longitudes as negative numbers.

```
location(tokyo, 35, -139).
location(rome, 41, -12).
location(london, 51, 0).
location(canberra, -35, -149).
location(madrid, 48, 3).
```

Now, to find out if one city is north of another, PROLOG needs only to get the latitude of both cities and then compare their sizes. One city will be north of another if the latitude of the first city is greater than the latitude of the second. Our student's PROLOG rule to do that looks like this:

```
north_of(X, Y) :-
    location(X, Lat1, _),
    location(Y, Lat2, _),
    Lat1 > Lat2.
```

To learn if Madrid is north of Tokyo one can enter north_of(Madrid, Tokyo), and PROLOG will respond with a "yes." The query north_of(City, tokyo) will cause PROLOG to report all cities north of Tokyo.

The rule to determine if a city is west of another is quite similar:

```
west_of(X, Y) :-
    location(X, _, Long1),
    location(Y, _, Long2),
    Long1 > Long2.
```

Queries to PROLOG using west_of are left to you.

PROLOG's arithmetic capabilities become more useful when they are applied to iterative processes. These are discussed in Chapters 4 and 5.

4
RECURSION AND RECURSIVE RULES

```
Once upon a time there was a story that went like this:

    Once upon a time there was a story that went like
        this:

        Once upon a time there was story that
            went like this:

                *    *    *    *

            And everyone lived happily ever
            after.

        And everyone lived happily ever after.

    And everyone lived happily ever after.
```

A process or definition (or story) is *recursive* if it uses or calls itself. The objective of a recursive process in a program is to repeatedly reduce the complexity of the problem until the solution is trivial. A popular example is the recursive solution to the towers of Hanoi problem. In that problem there are three pegs, one of which has a stack of successively smaller disks on it (see Figure 4.1). The objective is to move the stack from peg A to peg C subject to these rules:

1. Disks may only be moved from peg to peg.
2. Only one disk may be moved at a time.
3. The only disks that may be moved are the top disks on the pegs.
4. A disk may be placed only on the base level or on a larger disk.

You can solve the towers problem with this recursive algorithm: If n is the number of disks,

CHAPTER 4 RECURSION AND RECURSIVE RULES

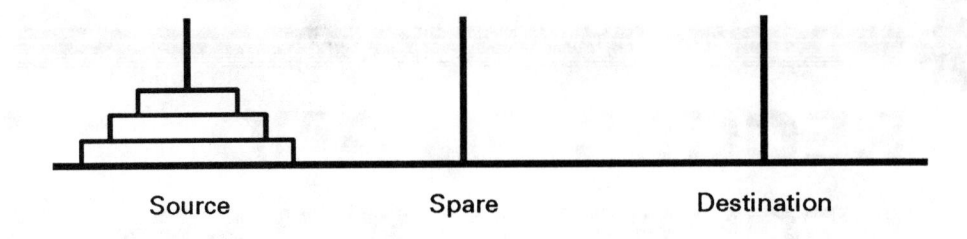

FIGURE 4.1 The Towers of Hanoi puzzle

1. Move n-1 disks from the source peg to the spare peg.
2. Move the bottom disk from the source peg to the destination peg.
3. Finally, move the n-1 disks from the spare peg to the destination peg.

What part of this procedure is recursive? When does the solution become trivial? How does one know when to stop moving the disks?

Recursion is the main repetitive control structure available in PROLOG. This chapter presents examples to illustrate its use. The final example is a PROLOG program that solves the towers of Hanoi puzzle using the algorithm from the previous paragraph.

4.1 RECURSION AS A GENERALIZATION OF NON-RECURSIVE RULES

One way to look at recursion is to consider it a generalization of a set of non-recursive rules. As an example, consider the set of rules that would define grandparent, great-grandparents, great-great-grandparents, and so on in our family database. Those rules might look like this:

```
grandparent(Ancestor, Descendant) :-
   parent(Ancestor, Person), parent(Person, Descendant).
greatgrandparent(Ancestor, Descendant) :-
   parent(Ancestor,Person), grandparent(Person,Descendant).
greatgreatgrandparent(Ancestor, Descendant) :-
   parent(Ancestor,Person), greatgrandparent(Person,Descendant).
```

Notice the pattern in the rules: The next ancestor in the sequence is the parent of the current ancestor. This recursive rule for ancestor captures that pattern:

```
ancestor(Ancestor, Descendant) :-
            parent(Ancestor, Person),
            ancestor(Person, Descendant).
```

This rule gives PROLOG all of the information it needs to find ancestors except for telling it that parents are ancestors. For that, we need an additional rule:

4.1 RECURSION AS A GENERALIZATION OF NON-RECURSIVE RULES

```
ancestor(Ancestor,Descendant) :-
        parent(Ancestor,Descendant).
```

A nonrecursive rule such as this one is necessary to allow PROLOG to stop the repetitive calls and find solutions to the goal, if any exist.

Listing 4.1 contains the family database of Listing 1.1 together with the ancestor and parent rules. If we address this query to PROLOG,

```
ancestor(Ancestor,Descendant) :-
    parent(Ancestor,Descendant).

ancestor(Ancestor, Descendant) :-
    parent(Ancestor, Person),
    ancestor(Person, Descendant).

parent(Parent, Child) :- mother_of(Parent, Child).
parent(Parent, Child) :- father_of(Parent, Child).

mother_of(edith, dick).
mother_of(edith, tom).
mother_of(sadie, calvin).
mother_of(sadie, alice).
mother_of(sadie, floyd).
mother_of(gertie, john_benford).
mother_of(gertie, edith).
mother_of(gertie, vivian).
mother_of(jane, luke).
mother_of(jane, sarah).
mother_of(jane, rachel).
mother_of(marcy, heidi).
mother_of(marcy, gretchen).
mother_of(linda, andrew).

step_father_of(tom, heidi).
step_father_of(tom, gretchen).

father_of(floyd, tom).
father_of(floyd, dick).
father_of(john_h, floyd).
father_of(john_h, calvin).
father_of(john_h, alice).
father_of(john_r, vivian).
father_of(john_r, edith).
father_of(john_r, john_benford).
father_of(john_benford, terri).
father_of(tom, luke).
father_of(tom, sarah).
father_of(tom, rachel).
father_of(tom, andrew).
```

LISTING 4.1 A family relationship database with an ancestor rule

CHAPTER 4 RECURSION AND RECURSIVE RULES

```
?- ancestor(sadie, sarah).
```

PROLOG will respond with "yes."

PROLOG follows these steps to determine the truth of the query:

1. Try the first ancestor rule instantiating arguments to `sadie` and `sarah`, respectively
    2. Call `parent(sadie, sarah)`.
        3. Check for `mother_of(sadie, sarah)` and fail.
        4. Check for `father_of(sadie, sarah)` and fail.
5. Try the second ancestor rule with the same arguments
    6. Call `parent(sadie, --)`
        7. Check `mother_of` list with `sadie` as first argument.
        8. Instantiate the second argument to the first of Sadie's children in the `mother_of` list = `calvin`
            9. Try the first ancestor rule with Calvin as Sarah's ancestor, `ancestor(calvin, sarah)`
            10. fail
            11. Try the second ancestor rule with Calvin as Sarah's ancestor, `ancestor(calvin, sarah)`
            12. fail
        13. Instantiate the second argument to Sadie's next child = `alice`
        14. fail (as with `calvin`)
        15. Instantiate the second argument to Sadie's next child = `floyd`
            16. Call `ancestor(floyd, sarah)` with first rule
            17. fail
            18. Call `ancestor(floyd, sarah)` with second rule
                19. Call `parent(floyd, --)`.
                    20. Call `mother_of(floyd, --)`.
                        21. fail
                    22. Call `father_of(floyd, -)`.
                        23. Instantiate second argument to `tom`
                            24. Call `ancestor(tom, sarah)` with first rule
                                25. Call `parent(tom, sarah)`
                                    26. Call `mother_of(tom, sarah)`
                                        27. fail
                                    28. Call `father_of(tom, sarah)`.

At that point, PROLOG has confirmed that Sadie is Sarah's ancestor and will report "yes." If we were to ask it to (by pressing the semicolon key), PROLOG would continue to search for other ways in which to confirm the relationship, but, for this database, would find none.

You can use the ancestor rules to find either ancestors or descendants or all possible combinations of the two. (Chapter 7 discusses the ordering of the clauses in the body of the rule to make it most efficient depending on whether it is finding descendants or ancestors.)

Stream Networks

The database in Listing 4.2 provides another example of a set of relationships that can be described recursively. The streams and the body of water into which they empty are identified with the relationship

```
tributary(Stream, Body_of_water).
```

Two rules called *drains_to* define the relationship that specifies all the bodies of water receiving the waters of a given stream:

```
drains_to(Stream, Body_of_water) :-
    tributary(Stream, Body_of_water).
drains_to(Stream, Body_of_water) :-
    tributary(Stream, Intermediate),
    drains_to(Intermediate, Body_of_water).
```

The second *drains_to* contains the recursive call and allows PROLOG to find the indirect tributaries. The first *drains_to* lets PROLOG find all of the situations listed in the tributary fact list and thus serves as a stopping condition for the recursion.

4.2 SUGGESTIONS FOR WRITING RECURSIVE RULE SETS

When writing recursive rules, put the stopping condition first. This ensures that PROLOG will evaluate the nonrecursive rule before generating another recursive call. Also, in the recursive rule, put the recursive predicate at the end of the body of the recursive rule. Recursion with the recursive call at the end of the rule is called *tail recursion*.

Following these suggestions will improve the efficiency of the rules and will, in some cases, prevent errors. To see how alternate arrangements can lead to errors, try switching the order of the two predicates in the body of the recursive drains_to rule in Listing 4.2. When you do that, PROLOG responds to the query

```
?- drains_to(hurricane_ck, Where).
```

```
drains_to(X, Y) :- tributary(X, Y).
drains_to(X, Z) :-
    tributary(X, Y),
    drains_to(Y, Z).

tributary(mississippi, gulf_of_mexico).
tributary(missouri, mississippi).
tributary(ohio, mississippi).
tributary(kanawha, ohio).
tributary(hurricane_ck, kanawha).
tributary(poplar_fork_ck, hurricane_ck).
tributary(eighteen_mile_ck, kanawha).
tributary(long_branch, poplar_fork_ck).
tributary(jakes_branch, eighteen_mile_ck).
tributary(sandusky, lake_erie).
```

LISTING 4.2 Stream networks

with the correct responses (kanawha, ohio, mississippi, and gulf_of_mexico) but continues in an endless loop. The loop never ends because as PROLOG evaluates the *drains_to* condition in the second *drains_to* rule, both arguments are uninstantiated, and PROLOG matches them with values from the database over and over.

Along with this advice on how to write recursive rules, we caution you to take care to avoid inadvertent recursion. You do this when you define a pair of rules in terms of one another. For example, one could define

```
brother(Boy,Girl) :- sister(Girl,Boy).
sister(Girl,Boy) :- brother(Boy,Girl).
```

You probably would never make such an obvious mistake, but this type of error becomes harder to recognize when there are more than two definitions in the cycle.

4.3 FINDING FACTORIAL VALUES

Mathematicians define the factorial of an integer as the product of the integer and all the integers less than it. Five factorial is

```
5 * 4 * 3 * 2 * 1 = 120
```

They also define 1 factorial to be (1 * zero factorial) and zero factorial to be 1. While you may seldom want to know the factorial of a number, the process of determining the value provides a classic illustration of the way recursion works in PROLOG.

This rule will return the correct value for zero factorial:

```
factorial(0,1) :- !.
```

4.3 FINDING FACTORIAL VALUES

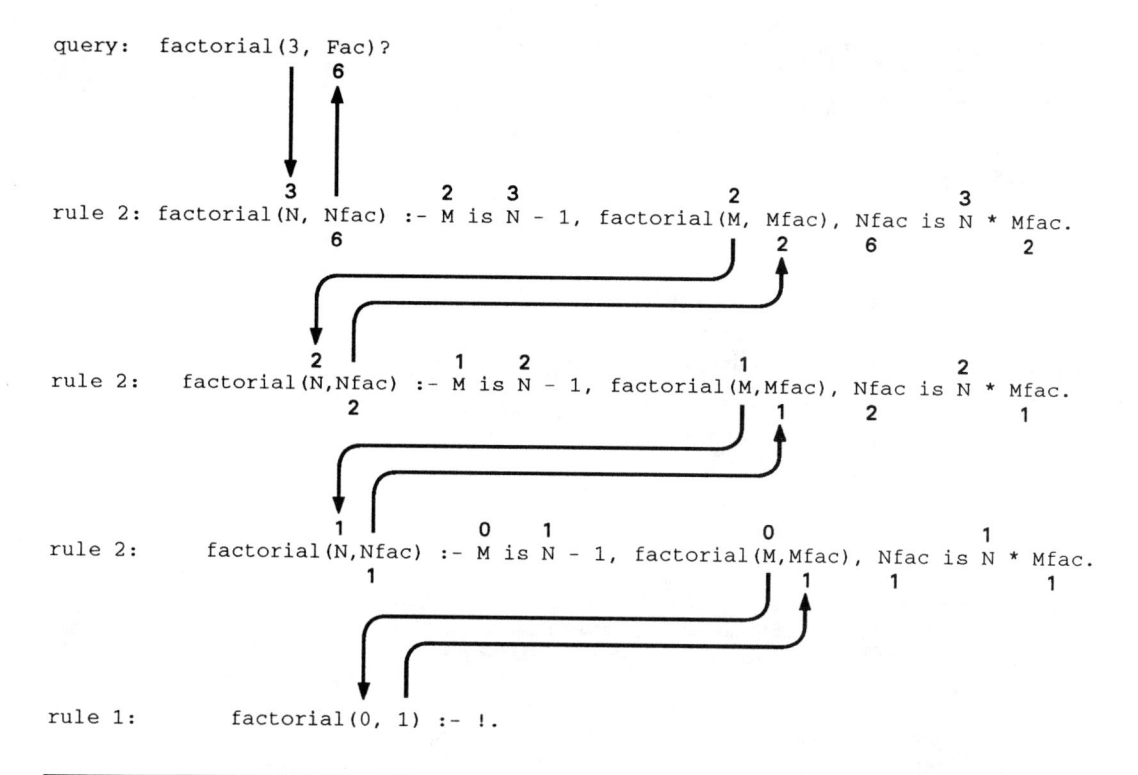

```
query:    factorial(3, Fac)?
                     6

                     3            2     3                    2                3
rule 2:   factorial(N, Nfac) :- M is N - 1, factorial(M, Mfac), Nfac is N * Mfac.
                     6                                       2     6                2

                     2            1     2                    1                2
rule 2:   factorial(N,Nfac) :- M is N - 1, factorial(M,Mfac), Nfac is N * Mfac.
                     2                                       1     2                1

                     1            0     1                    0                1
rule 2:   factorial(N,Nfac) :- M is N - 1, factorial(M,Mfac), Nfac is N * Mfac.
                     1                                       1     1                1

rule 1:   factorial(0, 1) :- !.
```

FIGURE 4.2 A query to *factorial*

Read it as saying that 0 factorial is 1. The body of the rule consists of just an exclamation point. The ! is a standard PROLOG symbol called the *cut*. In this instance, it instructs PROLOG to stop looking for other ways to satisfy the factorial rule. (Chapter 7 discusses use of the cut in more detail.)

By now, you may have an idea for a recursive algorithm for finding the other factorial values: For a number N, find the factorial of N-1 and multiply that value by N. In PROLOG we can write the rule this way:

```
factorial(N,Nfac):-        M is N - 1,
    factorial(M,Mfac),
    Nfac is N * Mfac.
```

Consider this interaction with PROLOG:

```
?- factorial(3,Factorial)
Factorial = 6
```

Figure 4.2 shows the steps that PROLOG followed to determine the value 6 for Nfac. The downward-pointing arrows show how values are passed for each recursive invocation of a rule, and the upward-pointing ones show the route of values passed back up the recursive chain.

```
hanoi(N) :- move(N, source, destination, spare).

report(X, Y) :-
    write('Move top disk from the '),
    write(X),
    write(' peg to the '),
    write(Y),
    write(' peg.'),
    nl.

move(0,_,_,_) :- !.

move(N, Source, Destination, Spare) :-
    M is N - 1,
    move(                   ),    % Algorithm step 1
    report(                 ),    %           step 2
    move(                   ).    %           step 3
```

```
?- hanoi(3).
Move top disk from the source peg to the destination peg.
Move top disk from the source peg to the spare peg.
Move top disk from the destination peg to the spare peg.
Move top disk from the source peg to the destination peg.
Move top disk from the spare peg to the source peg.
Move top disk from the spare peg to the destination peg.
Move top disk from the source peg to the destination peg.
```

LISTING 4.3 The Towers of Hanoi

4.4 THE TOWERS OF HANOI

The predicates defined in Listing 4.3 will solve the towers of Hanoi puzzle for whatever number of disks (N) you assign as an argument to the *hanoi* predicate.

There are two built-in predicates in the report rule that need some explanation. The *write* predicate sends the item enclosed in parentheses to the output stream. The other new term is *nl*. Inserted into the body of a rule, nl puts a carriage return in the output stream. The report rule produced the statements shown in the lower portion of Listing 4.3.

As with the previous examples, the recursive move procedure requires two rules. The first is the stopping condition that applies only when the number of disks to move is zero. The cut in this rule indicates that PROLOG should allow no more recursive calls now that the number of disks to move is zero.

The second move rule contains two recursive calls. These, together with the report rule, implement the algorithm in the introduction to this chapter. The algorithm's steps are:

1. Move n-1 disks from the source peg to the spare peg.
2. Move the bottom disk from the source peg to the destination peg.
3. Finally, move the n-1 disks from the spare peg to the destination peg.

Listing 4.3 does not list the arguments for the recursive calls; filling those in is left to you.

5 LISTS

Often you will want to work with a group of data items all at once. Examples of data to consider as a group are the children of Edith, the streams that flow into the Kanawha River, and cities with an average annual temperature of 14–16° C. In PROLOG you can manipulate data sets like these in lists.

A *list* is a data structure used especially for non-numeric processing and common to many programming languages. Consider a PROLOG list as having the same characteristics as a shopping list with one exception: A PROLOG list is an *ordered* sequence of elements while in our every day lists order is seldom important.

A list may contain constants, variables (which are used as place holders to be replaced with data later), structures, other lists, or a mixture of these. To write a list in PROLOG, name the elements in order and enclose them in square brackets, as in these examples:

```
[thom, dick, harry]
[Father, Mother, [Kids]]
[father_of(luke), mother_of(andrew)]
```

This chapter contains a general discussion of using PROLOG lists including an explanation of several PROLOG predicates for manipulating and evaluating lists.

5.1 REFERENCING LISTS

The procedures we have discussed so far do not allow you to reference the items in a PROLOG list. To illustrate the problem, consider this example of a data entry and query:

```
child_of(sadie, [alice, floyd, calvin]).
?- child_of(sadie, alice).
no
```

LIST	HEAD	TAIL
[alice, floyd, calvin]	alice	[floyd, calvin]
[soap,chips,[pop,beer,milk]	soap	[chips,[pop,beer,milk]]
[[chips,dip],[pop,beer]]	[chips,dip]	[[pop,beer]]
[milk]	milk	[]
[]	none	none
[a,b]	a	[b]
[a|b]	a	b

FIGURE 5.1 Lists, heads and tails

PROLOG responds to the query with no because it does not match alice in the query with the list in the fact. We begin this discussion of using lists with a description of the procedures for referencing the elements of a list.

Consider lists to have two parts: the first element, called the *head*, and the rest of the list, called the *tail*. The head of a list is not a list. The tail is a list containing every element of the original list except the first element. Figure 5.1 shows several examples of lists and identifies the head and tail of each.

Notice the empty brackets shown as the tail of the last list in Figure 5.1. The symbol [] represents a special list called the *empty list*. It is a part of all lists, and it differs from all other lists in that it has no head and no tail.

PROLOG syntax recognizes the vertical bar (|) as a separator of the head and tail of lists. To illustrate its use, look at this query about child_of relationships with sadie as the first argument:

```
?- child_of(sadie,[H|T]).
H = alice
T = [floyd, calvin]
```

PROLOG finds the fact in the database with sadie as the first argument and instantiates the second argument in the query to the second argument of the fact, [alice, floyd, calvin]. It then instantiates H to the first element in the list and T to the remainder of the list.

Figure 5.2 provides several examples of queries referencing a list. The last three reference both the head and tail of the list. Queries 4 and 5 reference the head of the tail of the list with the notation [H|[M| . . . where M indicates the element that is the head of the tail, or the second element in the list.

Notice that the fourth query causes PROLOG to respond with no. The response is negative because no list of children in the database of child_of

5.1 REFERENCING LISTS

These queries and responses are based on the following list of facts:

```
child_of(sadie, [alice, floyd, calvin]).
child_of(jane, [luke, sarah, rachel]).
child_of(edith, [dick, tom]).
child_of(linda, [butch, erica, elizabeth, eliot, andrew]).
```

1. ?- child_of(X, [luke, sarah, rachel]).
   X = jane

2. ?- child_of(X, [_,_,_]).
   X = sadie
   X = jane

3. ?- child_of(X, [H|T]).
   X = sadie
   H = alice
   T = [floyd, calvin]

   X = jane
   H = luke
   T = [sarah, rachel]

   X = edith
   H = dick
   T = [tom]

   X = linda
   H = butch
   T = [erica, elizabeth, eliot, andrew]

4. ?- child_of(X, [H|[M|rachel]]).
   no

5. ?- child_of(X, [H|[M|[rachel]]]).
   X = jane
   H = luke
   M = sarah

FIGURE 5.2 Queries referencing a list

relationships has the element rachel remaining after the first two elements are removed. What does remain after the first two elements are removed is the *list* [rachel] as query 5 confirms.

There is one PROLOG list that differs from all the others, the list referenced by [element1 | element2]. When this notation is used, with a constant following the vertical bar, the tail of the list is an element, not a list.

If the database contains `grocery_list([bread, beans])`, PROLOG will respond as follows:

```
?- grocery_list([Head | Tail]).
Head = bread
Tail = [beans]
```

This is the response we have seen before; the tail of the list is itself a list. However, look closely at this response to the query when the database fact is changed to `grocery_list([bread | beans])`:

```
?- grocery_list([Head | Tail]).
Head = bread
Tail = beans
```

For this case, the tail is not a list. The last list in Figure 5.1 is another example of this special list.

Referencing all of the items in a list is typically a recursive operation; queries 4 and 5 in Figure 5.2 exhibit the nested structure that lends itself to recursion. The process is to consider first the head of the list and then the head of the rest of the list. Most predicates that manipulate lists operate in this way. We consider several of these predicates, the first being one that confirms membership in a list.

5.2 EXAMINING THE ELEMENTS OF A LIST

It is often helpful to know a particular element is a member of a list. Is Vivian a child of Gertie? Does Hurricane Creek flow into the Kanawha River? Is IS 530 a core course for IS majors? PROLOG has a standard (but not usually built-in) predicate to answer questions like these. It is called member.

The Member Predicate

The *member* predicate determines if an element is in a list by first checking if that element is the head of the list and then checking if it is a member of the tail of the list. The PROLOG predicates to perform these two checks can be written like this:

```
member(X, [X|_]).
member(X, [_|Tail]) :- member(X, Tail).
```

The first member predicate confirms those cases of membership when the element is the head of the list. The second strips the head from the list and calls member again with the shortened list.

Notice how the notation causes PROLOG to remove the head for the recursive call. When you enter the query `member(cat, [dog, cat])`, what does PROLOG do? Figure 5.3 traces the calls and the instantiation of the variables as PROLOG tries to satisfy the query.

5.2 EXAMINING THE ELEMENTS OF A LIST

To satisfy the query member(cat, [dog, cat]), PROLOG begins by matching the query arguments with the arguments in the first member predicate:

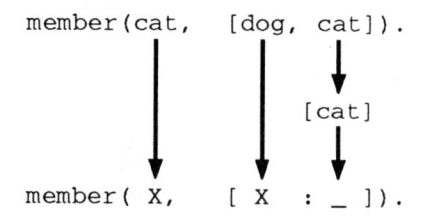

```
member(cat,   [dog, cat]).
   |           |     |
   |           |    [cat]
   |           |     |
   ▼           ▼     ▼
member( X,   [ X  :  _ ]).
```

This fails because cat and dog do not match. PROLOG then tries the second member predicate:

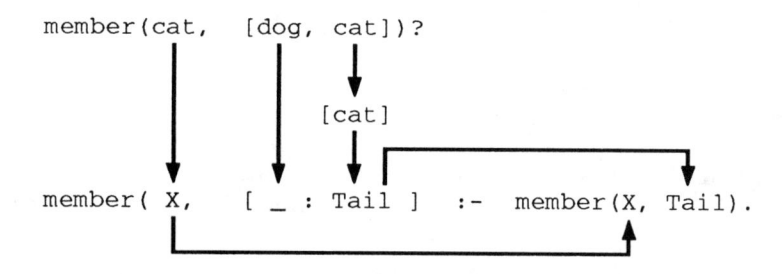

```
member(cat,   [dog, cat])?
   |           |     |
   |           |    [cat]
   |           |     |
   |           |     └──────────────┐
   ▼           ▼                    ▼
member( X,   [ _ : Tail ]  :-  member(X, Tail).
   └──────────────────────────────▲
```

Now PROLOG matches the arguments in the recursive call against the first predicate:

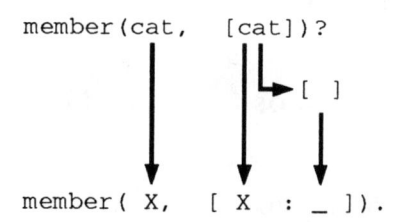

```
member(cat,  [cat])?
   |          |
   |          └─► [ ]
   |          |
   ▼          ▼
member( X,  [ X  :  _ ]).
```

Because cat matches with cat the goal succeeds, and PROLOG reports yes indicating that cat is a member of [dog, cat].

FIGURE 5.3 How *member* works

What happens after PROLOG finds a solution to satisfy the query goal? It keeps searching for more solutions. If the list were [dog, cat, cow, cat], PROLOG would report yes twice, once for each cat in the list. The process continues until the tail of the list becomes the empty list. When that happens, the recursive call is `member(X, [])`. The set of arguments in this call does not match the arguments in either of the two member predicates so the attempt to satisfy the goal fails (again) and PROLOG gives up the search.

Why does `member(X, [])` not match with the member predicates and thus stop the recursion? Remember the characteristics of the empty set. It has neither a head nor a tail and consequently cannot be divided into a head and a tail. This means the second arguments of both member predicates have a structure different from the second argument of the recursive call and a match is impossible.

Another question to consider is the effect of the member determination process on the original list. The original list remains unchanged; only the value to which the tail variable is instantiated changes.

Although we have defined *member* to be a predicate for determining membership in a list, you can use it in other ways. Suppose you wanted to show all the members of a list. Just query member like this:

```
?- member(X, [sue, sally, sid]).
X = sue ->;
X = sally ->;
X = sid ->;
```

Another, less obvious, but quite useful way you can use member is to find items common to more than one list. This compound query illustrates how to do that:

```
?- member(X, [sue, sally, sid]),
   member(X, [bill, coo, sue, sally, jack]).
X = sue ->;
X = sally ->;
no
```

In this case, the only X's reported are the ones that satisfy the membership test in both portions of the query.

Finding Elements in Specific Positions in a List

The first

What is a simple definition for a predicate that will return the first element in a list? Knowing that the first element is the head of the list and knowing how to reference the head of the list makes this definition simple:

```
first(X, [X | _]).
```

This query and response demonstrate the predicate:

```
?- first(First, [x, y, z]).
First = x
```

The second

Finding the second element is only slightly more complicated. We need to return the head of the tail. This predicate does that:

5.2 EXAMINING THE ELEMENTS OF A LIST

```
second(X, [_, X | _]).
```

This is an illustration of its use:

```
?- second(Second, [x, y, z]).  Second = y
```

The last

The technique we have been using makes it easy to find the third, fourth, and so on elements in a list, but what happens when we need the *last* element in a list and don't know ahead of time how many elements are in the list? If this problem sounds to you like it requires some recursion in the solution, you are right.

If there is only one element in the list, this predicate will return the answer:

```
last(X, [X]).
```

This will serve as the stopping condition. When there is more than one element in the list, we need only remove the head of the list repeatedly until just one element remains. This predicate will remove the heads, eventually making a list that matches the arguments in the first last predicate:

```
last(X, [_ | Tail]) :- last(X, Tail).
```

If we apply it to the x, y, z list it returns the last element:

```
?- last(Last, [x, y, z]).
Last = z
```

Counting List Elements

Counting the elements in a list requires PROLOG to remove successive heads just as it must do to find the last element in the list. In addition, there must be a clause to increment a counter each time a head is removed. This modification of the last/2 predicate does that:

```
count(Num, [_ | Tail]) :- count(Num2, Tail),
    Num is Num2 + 1.
```

There must also be a stopping condition. Since this predicate removes the heads from the list until there are no elements remaining, the empty list is an appropriate place to end the process. Enter this count rule *before* the recursive one:

```
count(0, []) :- !.
```

This illustrates a query to the count predicate and PROLOG's response:

```
?- count(Num_elements, [49, 17, 4]).
Num_elements = 3
```

Arity Prolog provides a built-in predicate to count the elements in a list. It is `length(List, Length)`. It works just like count/2.

```
?- length(Num_elements, [a, b, [c, d, e]]).
Num_elements = 3
```

Summing a List

Summing a list differs from counting it only in that the accumulator sums the elements of the list. This modified version of count, called sum_list, will find the sum of a list's elements:

```
sum_list(0, []) :- !.
sum_list(Sum, [Head | Tail]) :- sum_list(Sum2, Tail),
                                Sum is Head + Sum2.
```

5.3 FORMING NEW LISTS

PROLOG's list syntax makes it easy to add a new element to the head to a list. This predicate does that:

```
addhead(List, Element, [Element | List]).
```

A query to addhead/3 can get the new list:

```
?- addhead([a, b, c], x, Newlist).
Newlist = [x, a, b, c]
```

or it can get the old list:

```
?- addhead(Oldlist, x, [x, a, b, c]).
Oldlist = [a, b, c]
```

or it can get the element added to the old list to get the new list:

```
?- addhead([a, b, c], Element, [x, a, b, c]).
Element = x
```

The Append Predicate

The process of adding one list to the back of another is called *appending*. For example, suppose we had these two lists:

```
List1 = [ 'RI', 'WV', 'OR' ]
List2 = [ 'OH', 'MO']
```

Appending List2 to List1 will produce new List3:

```
List3 = [ 'RI', 'WV', 'OR', 'OH', 'MO']
```

The standard PROLOG predicate known as append/3 performs this operation:

```
append([], List2, List2).
append([Head | Tail1], List2, [Head | Tail3]) :-
       append(Tail1, List2, Tail3).
```

5.3 FORMING NEW LISTS

The standard definition of append:

```
append([], List, List).

append([ Head | Tail1 ], List2, [ Head | Tail3]) :-
       append(Tail1, List2, Tail3).
```

```
query:         append([a,b], [c,d], Newlist)?

head:          append([a|b], [c,d], [a|Tail3])
                                              [b,c,d]

condition:     append([b], [c,d], Tail3)

head:          append([b|[]], [c,d], [b|Tail3_1])
                                              [c,d]

condition:     append([], [c,d], Tail3_1)

stopping rule: append([], [c,d], [c,d])
```

FIGURE 5.4 An example of appending

The first statement says that if the first list is empty, the result is just the second list. The second append/3 statement says that to append List2 to List1 to form List3, put the head of List1 at the head of List3 and append the two tails.

Figure 5.4 traces the instantiation of the variables in the recursive process of appending the list [c, d] to the list [a, b] to form the new list [a, b, c, d].

Append/3, like addhead/3, can be used in different ways. You already know how to use it to form a new list. You can also use it to determine what needs to be added to the front of a list to give a particular result, as in this example:

```
?- append(Front, [c, d], [a, b, c, d]).
Front = [a, b]
```

Another possibility is to use it to truncate a list of a specified front portion:

```
?- append([a, b], Truncated_list, [a, b, c, d]).
Truncated_list = [c, d]
```

Still another way to use it is to find all the possible combinations of List1 and List2 that will produce List3:

```
?- append(List1, List2, [a, b, c, d]).
List1 = []
List2 = [a, b, c, d]

List1 = [a]
List2 = [b, c, d]   and so on.
```

5.4 OTHER LIST PREDICATES

There are many possible list manipulations for which built-in predicates exist or for which you can write a predicate. This section describes just two, one which determines if an object is a list and one which allows conversion between lists and PROLOG facts.

Recognizing a List

How can PROLOG recognize a list? The problem is not complicated, but it is perhaps not so simple as it appears at first thought. As a first try, isa-list([List]) might seem to work. It does, but only for a one-element list. The empty list and lists with more than one-element are not recognized as lists.

One way to recognize all lists is to use a recursive procedure that removes the head successively until only the empty list remains:

```
is_list([]).
is_list([Head | Tail]) :- is_list(Tail).
```

This will recognize lists including the empty list. It will also reject lists with the special form [head|tail] because the tail is not a list. One problem with this set of rules is that the query is_list(X) will cause it to loop infinitely. Infinite loops can be prevented by adding the following clause before the other two:

```
is_list(X) :- var(X), !, fail.
```

This tells PROLOG that an uninstantiated variable is not a list.

The Univ Predicate

Many versions of PROLOG, including Arity, have a built-in predicate called *univ* that is represented in PROLOG syntax with the symbol =.. This predicate

5.4 OTHER LIST PREDICATES

forms lists from PROLOG clauses and creates PROLOG clauses out of lists. This is an example of turning a list into a clause:

```
?- Clause =.. [likes, jack, peanut_butter].
Clause = likes(jack, peanut_butter)
```

In response to this query PROLOG returns a list:

```
?- likes(jack, peanut_butter) =.. List.
List = [likes, jack, peanut_butter]
```

You will find univ useful when you begin writing PROLOG programs that modify themselves.

6
INPUT AND OUTPUT

This chapter explains the most often used built-in predicates for input and output.[1] Because PROLOG programs often must report lists of information found in a database, the standard PROLOG predicates for forming and printing such lists are also explained in this chapter. The chapter concludes with an introduction to Arity Prolog's database-manipulation predicates.

Three short applications programs illustrate the use of the built-in predicates. Listing 6.1 creates a simple interactive menu system. Listing 6.2 reads a sentence from the keyboard and creates a list of each word and punctuation mark entered by the user. Listing 6.3, reads a text file and displays it on the screen.

```
go :-
    cls,
    display_menu,
    read_inquiry_type(Type),
    find_goal(Type,Goal),
    call(Goal),
    nl,nl,nl,
    write('Do you want to query the family database again? (y/n)   '),
    read_string(3,StringResponse),
    string_term(StringResponse, Response),
    continue(Response).

find_goal(1, one).
find_goal(2, two).
find_goal(3, three).
find_goal(4, four).
find_goal(5, five).
```

LISTING 6.1 (Continues next page)

---

1 I/O predicates vary greatly among PROLOG implementations, so be sure to test them on the system you will use to run your application.

```
continue(Response) :-
    member(Response, ['Y', y, 'YES', 'Yes', yes]),
    go,
    !.

continue(Response) :-
    cls,
    nl, nl, nl,
    write('  Thanks for using the family database inquiry program.').

display_menu :-
    nl,
    write('        FAMILY DATABASE INQUIRIES'),
    nl,nl,
    write('Enter the number of the type of inquiry you wish to make.'),
    nl,nl,nl,
    write('        1. Find the children of a person'), nl,
    write('        2. Find the parents of a person'), nl,
    write('        3. Find the grandparents of a person'), nl,
    write('        4. Find the grandchildren of a person'), nl,
    write('        5. Quit this program'),
    nl,nl,
    write('The type of inquiry you wish to make is number:   ').

read_inquiry_type(Type) :-
    read_string(1,StringType),
    string_term(StringType, Type).

one :-
    nl,
    write('For what person do you want a list of children?  '), nl,
    read_string(20, StringPerson),
    string_term(StringPerson, Person),
    nl,
    write('This is a list of the children of '),
    write(Person),
    write(':  '), nl,
    find_children(Person).

find_children(Person) :-
    find_it(Child, parent(Person, Child), Childlist),
    printlist(Childlist).

printlist( [] ).
printlist( [Head | Tail] ):-
    tab(5),
    write(Head),
    printlist(Tail).
```

LISTING 6.1 A family database query menu (continued)

```
read_sentence([Word|Word_list]) :-
            write('Enter a sentence.'), nl,
            get0(Ch),
            name(Char1, [Ch]),
            readword(Char1, Word, Char2),
            restsent(Word, Char2, Word_list).

restsent(Word, _, []) :- lastword(Word), !.

restsent(Word, Char1, [Word1|Word_list]) :-
            readword(Char1, Word1, Char2),
            restsent(Word1, Char2, Word_list).

readword(Ch, Word, Ch1) :-
            one_char_word(Ch), !,
            Word = Ch,
            get0(C),
            name(Ch1, [C]).

readword(Ch, Word, Ch2) :-
            inword(Ch, NewChar), !,
            get0(C),
            name(Ch1, [C]),
            restword(Ch1, Char_list, Ch2),
            Word = [NewChar | Char_list].

readword(Ch, Word, Ch2) :-
            get0(C),
            name(Ch1, [C]),
            readword(Ch1, Word, Ch2).

restword(Ch, [NewCh|Char_list], Ch2) :-
            inword(Ch, NewCh), !,
            get0(C),
            name(Ch1, [C]),
            restword(Ch1, Char_list, Ch2).

restword(Ch, [], Ch).

inword(Char, NewChar) :-
            "Char" = [26],
            NewChar = ''.

inword(Char, Char) :-
            Char @>= 'a', Char @=< 'z'.
```

LISTING 6.2 (Continues next page)

```
inword(Char, LCChar) :-
            Char @>= 'A', Char @=< 'Z',
            name(Char, [Ascii]),
         NewAscii is Ascii + 32,
         name(LCChar, [NewAscii]).

inword(Char, Char) :-
            Char @>= '0', Char @=< '9'.

inword(Char, Char) :-
            Char = ''''.

inword(Char, Char) :-
            Char = '-'.


lastword('.').
lastword('!').
lastword('?').


one_char_word('.').
one_char_word(',').
one_char_word(';').
one_char_word(' ').
one_char_word(':').
one_char_word('?').
one_char_word('!').
one_char_word('''').
```

LISTING 6.2 Reading a sentence (continued)


```
go :-
    write('Enter the name of the file to display:  '),
    read_string(12, FileName),
    open(H, FileName ,r),
    read_file(H, Line),
    close(H).

read_file(H, Line) :-
    read_line(H, Line),
    nonvar(Line),
    write(Line), nl,
    read_file(H, NextLine).

read_file(H, Line).
```

Listing 6.3 A program to display a text file

6.1 READING AND WRITING

Figure 6.1 contains four input predicates: read/1, get0/1, get/1, and read_string/2. The read/1 predicate reads a term from the standard input device (usually the keyboard). PROLOG recognizes the end of the term when it reads a period followed by the Enter key, although it does not include the period as a part of the term. This is an example using read/1:

```
?- read(X).
butterfly.
X = butterfly
```

READING AND WRITING TERMS

- `read(X)`   Reads X from the current input stream; if the current input stream is the console, X must terminate with a period and a carriage return.

- `write(X)`   Writes X to the current output stream. X can be a term, string, list, or structure. Must be a separate write predicate for each item.

- `writeq(X)`   Writes X to the current output stream, quoting it when it begins with an upper-case letter or contains spaces.

READING AND WRITING CHARACTERS

- `get0(X)`   Gets the next character from the current input stream.

- `get(X)`   Gets the next printable character from the current input stream; non-printable characters are ignored.

- `put(X)`   Puts the character X into the current output stream.

READING STRINGS

- `read_string/2`   read_string(MaxStrLength, String) reads a string of maximum length = MaxStrLength from the current input stream.

MISCELLANEOUS PREDICATES

- `nl`   Puts a line feed into the output stream.

- `tab(N)`   If N is an integer, tab(N) puts N spaces into the output stream.

FIGURE 6.1 Input/output predicates

The get0/1 predicate reads one character at a time. It is especially useful for reading and parsing sentences, because a parsing program must examine each individual character including spaces and punctuation to know what to do. Also, get0/1 is useful for reading the scan codes from function and arrow keys. If the argument to get0/1 is instantiated, get0/1 will return true if the argument and the character match; otherwise it will return false. Because get0/1 reads a single character, it is not necessary (or possible) to enter a period before PROLOG reads the character. The following code illustrates the use of get0/1:

```
?- get0(X).
a
X = 97 ->
```

The get/1 predicate also reads one character from the standard input device, but it skips any non-printing characters (ASCII codes < 32) like the form feed, the bell, and a space. When a printing character is entered, get/1 will produce the same results as get0/1; compare this example with the previous one:

```
?- get(X).
a
X = 97 ->
```

In the next example you can count the number of non-printing characters entered before the letter by noting the position on the line where the letter is echoed:

```
?- get(X).
      a
X = 97 ->
```

In Arity Prolog you can read strings with the built-in predicate read_string/2. This predicate's first argument is the maximum length of the string to be read, and its second argument represents the string. The following example illustrates its use; note that the string can include the carriage return and line feed symbols.

```
?read_string(40, X).
One, Two, Three, Go!
X = $One, Two, Three, Go!$ ->
```

Notice how, in the previous example, Arity Prolog surrounded the string with dollar signs. The dollar sign is the symbol that Arity uses to denote the beginning and end of string. An empty string is indicated by $$. To include a dollar sign in a string, enter two dollar signs as in $The cost is $$4.98.$.

Figure 6.1 also contains three output predicates. The write/1 predicate writes a term, a string, a list, or a structure to the output stream as does writeq/1. For example:

```
?- write([butch, erica, elizabeth, eliot, andrew]).
[butch, erica, elizabeth, eliot, andrew]
```

The difference between the two write predicates is that writeq/1 places the item in quotes if it begins with an upper-case letter or contains spaces. You must use a separate write or writeq for each item being written.

The put/1 predicate writes a single character into the output stream.

Two other terms in Figure 6.1 help format output. Use nl/0 to put a carriage return and line feed into the output stream, and use tab/1 to put spaces into the output stream. Both are used as separate goals and not as arguments to the output predicates. For example, the following code will indent five spaces, write "Hello, Eliot!," skip a line, and write "How are you?"

```
?- tab(5),writeq('Hello, Eliot!'), nl,
   write('How are you?').
      'Hello, Eliot!'
How are you?
```

6.2 DATABASE MANIPULATION PREDICATES

PROLOG differs from most programming languages in that PROLOG programs can change themselves. Figure 6.2 lists single-argument Arity Prolog predicates that can change the contents of a database.

The first two read the contents of a file of PROLOG clauses and append them to any clauses already in the database. Sometimes you may have clauses

`consult(FName)`	Reads clauses from the file and places the clauses in the database.
`reconsult(FName)`	Performs the same process as *consult/1* except it replaces any duplicate definitions with the definition from the file.
`asserta(Clause)`	Adds the clause to the beginning of the list of clauses of the same name.
`assertz(Clause)`	Adds the clause to the end of the list of clauses of the same name.
`assert(Clause)`	Performs the same function as *assertz*.
`retract(Clause)`	Removes a single clause from the database; the predicate name must be specified.
`abolish(Name/Arity)`	Removes all clauses from the database with the specified name and arity.

FIGURE 6.2 Database manipulation predicates

RULE	FUNCTION

`find_it(X, G, _) :-`
`    call(G),`
`    asserta(found(X)),`
`    fail.`
	Creates a list of facts in the database of the form: *found*(X). Each X satisfies the goal G.

`find_it(_, _, L) :-`
`    list_it([], L),`
`    !.`
	Call *list_it*/2 to form the list, L.

`list_it(S, L) :-`
`    retract(found(X)),`
`    list_it([X|S], L).`
	Retracts the *found*(X) facts from the database as it adds the X's to the head of the list. Fails when there are no more *found*(X)'s to retract.

`list_it(L, L).`	The stopping condition for *list_it*; tried and succeeds when the first rule fails.

FIGURE 6.3 Building lists from the database

in the file with the same name and arity as are already in the database. To avoid placing duplicates of the clauses into the database, use reconsult/1 rather than consult/1; reconsult/1 will replace any duplicate definitions with the definition being read from the file.

To write a rule that adds clauses to the database, use one of the assert predicates. Two of them, assert/1 and assertz/1, add the clause to the end of the list of clauses of the same name in the database; asserta/1 adds the clause to the beginning of the list of clauses of the same name. The find_it/3 rule in Figure 6.3 uses asserta/1 to insert a list of facts into the database.

The last two predicates remove clauses from a database. Use retract/1 to remove one clause. To remove all clauses with the same name and arity, use abolish/1. The list_it/2 predicate in Figure 6.3 uses retract/1 to remove a clause from the database as it inserts the clause's argument into a list of items.

6.3 INPUT AND OUTPUT EXAMPLES

This section discusses some common input and output tasks and demonstrates built-in predicates from Figure 6.1.

Forming a List From Information in a Database

The most convenient way to report information found in a database is first to put the items in a list and then to print the list. The-children-of-Edith and streams-that-flow-into-the-Ohio-River as found in the family (Listing 4.1) and stream (Listing 4.2) databases respectively, are examples of items that might go into such a list.

The Clocksin and Mellish names for the predicates that form a list this way are *findall/3* and *collect_found/2*. Figure 6.3 contains a slightly modified pair of rules, find_it/3 and list_it/2. Figure 6.3 also describes what each rule does. You could use find_it/3 to query the family database to get a list of a person's children this way:

```
?- find_it(Child, parent(sadie, Child), Childlist).
Childlist = [calvin, alice, floyd]
```

Printing a List

You can always write a list in list form with the brackets, but users are likely to prefer having elements printed individually. This set of rules will do that:

```
printlist( [] ).
printlist( [Head | Tail] ) :- tab(5),
                              write(Head), nl,
                              printlist(Tail).
```

This query shows how it works:

```
?- printlist([jim, bob, jones]).
     jim
     bob
     jones
```

This rule set is easy to tailor to your specific needs. To cause the list to print in reverse order, just reverse the order of the last two conditions of the second rule. This example illustrates what happens when you make that change:

```
?- printlist2([jim, bob, jones]).
     jones
     bob
     jim
```

In addition, you might need to add some end-of-list punctuation to the first rule or omit the nl/0 predicate so that all elements of the list are on a single line.

Creating a Menu

Menus are an easy way for users to select among program options. Listing 6.1 illustrates the structure of a program that allows people unfamiliar with PROLOG to query a family database. In addition to the rules shown there, the program uses the member/2, printlist/1, find_it/3, and list_it/2 predicates.

The first rule, go, starts the program and directs it: The built-in predicate *cls* clears the screen. Successive predicates print the menu on the screen (display_menu), read the user's choice of query type (read_inquiry_type(Type)), translate the type number into a word that can be a PROLOG predicate (find_goal(Type, Goal)), perform the appropriate query (call(Goal)), prompt the user about another query (write/1) and read the response (read_string(3,StringResponse)), and, finally, evaluate that response (continue(Response)).

Only one of the query types is implemented in this example. One/0 asks the user the name of the person whose children are sought (print) and reads the name (read_string(20, StringPerson)). After printing a title (write/1), it calls find_children(Person), to get and print the list of children. Find_children/1 uses the find_it/3 and printlist/1 rules discussed above.

Once the program displays the response to the query, it asks if the user wants answers to other questions. The first continue/1 rule determines if the user's response to the prompt is a member of the set of continue responses. If it is, this rule begins the program again by calling go/0. If it is not, the first continue/1 rule fails and the second one succeeds, clears the screen, prints a farewell message, and turns on the prompt.

Listing 6.1 needs a lot of work before it would be very useful, and it can be enhanced in many ways. Predicates to implement inquiry types 2–5 are missing, and additional inquiry types would make the program more useful. People unfamiliar with PROLOG are likely to enter names with an upper-case first letter; converting to lower-case would avoid problems. Also, the list of names printed by the program would look more natural if the first letter of each name were in upper-case. Finally, a query category that would allow direct PROLOG queries to the database would add a nice touch.

Reading Sentences

Listing 6.2 contains a program to form a list of the words and punctuation that comprise a sentence entered from the keyboard.

The inword/2 predicate screens all characters that can come from the keyboard and accepts for the program only those that are allowed in a sentence. The first inword/2 reads the end of file character and converts it to a null character. The third inword/2 predicate converts all upper-case characters to their lower-case equivalent.

The one_char_word/1 facts screen incoming characters and identify those that are words in themselves, the comma, period, and so on. The lastword/1 facts identify the three one-character words that signal the end of a sentence, the period, exclamation point, and question mark.

Read_sentence/1 is the driving predicate. It obtains the list of words and punctuation that make up the sentence. It gets the first character in the input stream, reads the first word, and then gets the rest of the sentence.

There are three readword/3 predicates. The first is for one-character words; it converts the character from a list to a word and then gets the next character. The second one does most of the work in ordinary sentences. It checks to see if a character is usable. If it is usable, this readword/3 performs the necessary character conversions, gets the next character, obtains the rest of the word, puts the new character at the head of the character list, and converts the character list to a word string. The final readword is for characters that are not allowable in a sentence. It simply ignores the current character and continues by getting the next character and then the rest of the word.

The first restword/3 predicate checks to see if a character is acceptable, and, if it is, puts it at the head of the character list, and gets the next character and the rest of the word. The second restword is for lastword characters. It returns a second character that is the same as the first and an empty character list.

The first restsent/3 predicate is also for lastword characters. When these characters are detected, this restsent/3 predicate stops looking for more of the sentence. The second restsent/3 predicate reads a word and then reads the rest of the sentence.

6.4 FILE I/O

The predicates for writing to files are similar to those I/O predicates discussed previously. The only difference is an additional first argument that instantiates to the system assigned number (called a *handle*) associated with the file. Figure 6.4 lists the file I/O versions of the predicates. You can use the file I/O predicates with the standard I/O devices by specifying a handle = 0.

Before you can read from or write to a file you must open it. The predicate open/3 opens a file. The first argument to open/3 is the file handle.[2] The second argument represents the file name and should be instantiated to a valid DOS file name. The third argument denotes the mode in which the file is to be accessed. Figure 6.4 lists the five possible access modes.

If the file you are going to use does not exist, you must create it. The create/2 predicate will create a file, open it for writing, and assign a handle.

A third predicate for opening files is p_open/3. It will open a file just like open/3, but, in addition to searching the current directory for the file, it will look for the filename in the directory of the .exe file of the current application and then in the directories listed in the path command of the autoexec.bat file.

After your program is finished using a file, the file should be closed. This is important so that your programs do not attempt to have more files open at one time than your system allows. To close a file, use close/1. It will close the file with the specified handle.

---

[2] Because the system assigns this number, it is not important to know what the number is. You must, however, take care that you do not confuse one file with another by mixing up the handle references.

PREDICATES FOR INPUT/OUTPUT

All of the i/o predicates in Figure 6.1 are available with an additional argument (the first) that indicates a file handle. In that form, they read from or write to the file with the specified handle. The predicates in this form are listed below. Also listed is the *read_line*/2 predicate which reads a full line of text from a text file. As with the other file I/O predicates, you can use it to read from the keyboard by using 0 for the handle argument.

```
read(H, Term)     get0(H, Char)    read_string(H, MaxL, S)    tab(H, N)
write(H, Term)    get(H, Char)     read_line(H, Line)         nl(H)
writeq(H, Term)   put(H, Char)
```

FILE MANIPULATION PREDICATES

The access mode for which files may be opened and the symbol to use in the *open* and *p_open* predicates are:

read	r	read or write	rw
write	w	read or append	ra
append	a		

`create(H, Fname)`   Opens a new file for writing. H becomes instantiated to the system assigned integer value of the file handle. If the file name contains characters other than letters and integers or begins with an upper-case letter, it must be enclosed in single quotes.

`open(H, Fname, Access)`   Opens file with the specified access mode.

`p_open(H, Fname, Access)`   Opens the file as does open, but, in addition to the current directory, searches (1) the directory of the *.exe* file of the current application, and then (2) the directories listed in the *path* command of the *autoexec.bat* file.

`close(H)`   Closes the file with the specified handle.

FIGURE 6.4 Predicates for file I/O

A File I/O Example

Listing 6.3 will read and display a text file. It first asks the user for the name of the file to use; the read_string predicate gets the file name. Next the file is opened for reading. The read_file/2 rule reads and displays the file. It reads each line of the file with the read_line/2 predicate. The nonvar/1 predicate is a check to see that a line has been read. If nonvar succeeds, the line is displayed by write/1, and there is a recursive call to read_file/2.

When nonvar/1 fails, the second read_file/2 succeeds and then execution resumes in the go/0 rule where the file is closed and the program ends.

7
PROGRAM CONTROL AND PROGRAM DESIGN

There are at least two ways to view a PROLOG program. You can consider the program to be a database that describes some limited world. Alternatively, you can consider the program as a series of directions to PROLOG. The first of these perspectives leaves to PROLOG all concerns about how the program operates. However, at times you may be very concerned about exactly what PROLOG does and when it does it. So far, with the exception of a few comments introducing the cut, we have said little about controlling execution in a PROLOG program.

In this chapter we turn our attention to the workings of PROLOG programs. The first portion of the chapter examines ways to control execution. The chapter's other main topic is program design.

7.1 CONTROLLING PROGRAM EXECUTION

There are a variety of steps you can take to control program execution. In this section we discuss the order of clauses in rules and the cut (!).

Clause Arrangement

You can increase the efficiency of your rules by putting the predicate with the fewest possible matches first. As an example, consider this rule, which determines if a menu is acceptable to Willi:

```
meal_for_willi(Main_course, Beverage) :-
    willi_eats(Main_course),
    willi_drinks(Beverage).
```

The best arrangement for the clauses in the rule depends on the database. If there are relatively few main courses compared to beverages, the above arrangement is the one to use. On the other hand, if the database has many more main courses than beverages, the rule will run quicker if the beverages are tested first.

A similar bit of advice is to arrange entries in a fact set so that the ones to be used most often are listed at the top. When it is appropriate, you could have your program keep active data items at the top of the database list by retracting facts and then asserting them at the top of the fact list like this:

```
meal_for_willi(Main_course, Beverage) :-
    willi_eats(Main_course),
    willi_drinks(Beverage),
    !,
    retract(willi_eats(Main_course),
    asserta(willi_eats(Main_course).
```

Of course, you would want to do this only for very large fact lists and for queries like this one, which has a constant for each argument:

```
meal_for_willi(spaghetti, chocolate_milkshake).
```

Another, somewhat more practical example that illustrates the importance of clause arrangements is the grandparent/2 predicate:

```
grandparent(Grandparent, Grandchild) :-
    parent(Grandparent, Parent),
    parent(Parent, Grandchild).
```

This version of grandparent/2 is efficient at responding to queries like

```
grandparent(gertie, Grandchild).
```

In responding, PROLOG will instantiate Grandparent to `gertie`, perform the necessary steps to instantiate the Parent argument in `parent(gertie, Parent)`, and then find those arguments that cause the goal `parent(Parent, Grandchild)` to succeed.

Notice how much more work PROLOG would have to do if the two conditions in the rule were reversed: Instead of just finding the children of Gertie's children, it would test every parent-child combination to see if the child were Gertie's grandchild!

This same inefficiency occurs when you use this rule to find the grandparent of an individual as in this query:

```
grandparent(Grandparent, rachel).
```

To respond to queries of this type, this form of the grandparent rule is much more efficient

```
grandparent2(Grandparent, Grandchild) :-
    parent(Parent, Grandchild),
    parent(Grandparent, Parent).
```

When you have rules like these that may be used for different types of queries, and clause order affects efficiency, consider having separate predicates for each query type. In this case, you could have two predicates, grandchild/2 for finding grandchildren, and grandparent/2 for finding grandparents. Be sure to arrange the clauses so that the clause with the fewest possible matches appears first.

One bit of advice we offered in Chapter 4 was to put the recursive call at the end of a rule wherever possible. This form of recursion is called *tail recursion*. A tail-recursive rule is more efficient than other recursive rules in many PROLOG implementations because they provide for *tail-recursion* (also called *last-call*) *optimization*.

The requirements for tail-recursion optimization are these:

1. The recursive call is in the last clause of the predicate.
2. The call is the last subgoal of the clause.
3. There are no untried alternatives for earlier subgoals in the clause.

This example of a rule that displays numbers beginning at N and ending at Limit satisfies the conditions:

```
count(N, Limit) :-  N =< Limit,
                    write(N),
                    nl,
                    NewN is N + 1,
                    count(NewN, Limit).
```

Unfortunately, more often than not, the third condition for tail recursion optimization will be very difficult to meet. In the discussion of the cut that follows, we provide an example that uses the cut and some extra arguments to allow a recursive rule to meet that condition.

Using the Cut (!) to Control Program Execution

You have seen the cut, written as !, in some of the previous chapters' rule examples. The cut is a goal that succeeds automatically, but only once. Whenever backtracking causes a return to the cut, the cut fails and so does its parent rule.

The cut thus gives you the ability to restrict PROLOG to evaluating clauses in a rule only one time. As an example, consider the first restword/3 predicate from Listing 6.2:

```
restword(Ch, [NewCh|Char_list], Ch2) :-
        inword(Ch, NewCh),
        !,
        get0(C),
        name(Ch1, [C]),
        restword(Ch1, Char_list, Ch2).
```

PROLOG will evaluate the clauses following the cut with the set of variables that were instantiated prior to the cut. The cut fences off any backtracking above (to the left of) it. However, be sure to notice that it has no effect on goals that follow it in a rule.

There are three reasons for using the cut. One is efficiency; you can use the cut to make your programs run faster by avoiding attempts to satisfy a goal that cannot contribute to a solution. The cut after the stopping conditions in recursive-rule sets usually serves this purpose. These rules to sum the first N numbers provide an illustration:

```
sum_to(1,1) :- !.
sum_to(N, Sum) :- N1 is N - 1,
         sum_to(N1, Sum1),
         Sum is Sum1 + N.
```

The cut in the first rule tells PROLOG not to bother trying the second rule when N is 1.

However, there is another way to prevent PROLOG from executing all of the second rule when N is 1: add N > 1 as the first clause in the second rule. With that clause in place, the cut in the first rule is unnecessary. We prefer this alternative because it makes the second definition of sum_to complete.

A second reason to use the cut is to prevent duplicate answers. Suppose you want to know if two lists have at least one common member. As you saw in Chapter 5, the member/3 predicate provides an easy way to determine that:

```
common_member(X, List1, List2) :-
     member(X, List1),
     member(X, List2).
```

However, if all you need to determine is the existence of one element in common, this predicate does more than is necessary. You can make it more efficient by stopping it when the common membership of an element is confirmed. Adding a cut after the second member/3 predicate does that:

```
common_member(X, List1, List2) :-
     member(X, List1),
     member(X, List2),
     !.
```

A third reason to use the cut is to stop PROLOG's search after it has found the only possible answer. For this purpose, the cut is often used with another built-in predicate, fail. *Fail* is a goal that always fails; it prevents PROLOG from examining another version of the rule that contains it.

To illustrate this situation, assume you are working on a database for St. Peter. In the database are predicates for sins and good works for each individual who has performed them. These are some examples:

7.1 CONTROLLING PROGRAM EXECUTION

```
shared_with_needy(alice).
shared_with_needy(lars).
shared_with_needy(billy_joe).
hot_fudge_twice_every_day(randolph).
hot_fudge_twice_every_day(juliette).
```

St. Peter wants a program that will let him enter the name of each soul that approaches the pearly gates and quickly determine if that person has performed some minimum level of good works and avoided some specific set of sins. After making that determination, he wants the program to simply tell him yes or no.

PROLOG can avoid a lot of needless searching of the database if it immediately rules out individuals who have committed unacceptable acts. Suppose the predicate that evaluates the candidates is called enter; you can write a first rule that immediately excludes a person like this:

```
enter(Person) :-
    hot_fudge_twice_every_day(Person),
    !,
    fail.
```

Whenever the hot-fudge goal succeeds the enter/1 rule fails, and PROLOG will not try any of its other versions. This is an example of a query and response:

```
?- enter(randolph).
no
```

Another example using the cut-fail combination is the definition for PROLOG's built-in predicate *not/1*:

```
not(Whatever) :- Whatever,
                !,
                fail.
not(Whatever).
```

This will cause failure if Whatever succeeds and cause success otherwise.

Not/1 can often be used instead of the cut-fail combination. In the enter/1 rule, you can write:

```
enter(Person) :-
    not(hot_fudge_twice_every_day(Person)),
    . . . .
```

Enter/1 will fail whenever Person is instantiated to a value that matches the argument in the hot_fudge_twice_every_day/1 fact list. We recommend this approach rather than the use of the cut because it makes the enter rule easier to understand.

A Tail-Recursive Factorial Predicate

The cut can help you to write a tail-recursive rule set for calculating factorials. The factorial rule in Chapter 4 is this:

```
factorial(0,1) :- !.
factorial(N, Nfac) :- M is N - 1,
                      factorial(M, Mfac),
                      Nfac is N * Mfac.
```

The second rule is not tail recursive because it fails condition (1). Making the recursive call as the last condition of the recursive rule requires some additional arguments so that PROLOG doesn't try to do arithmetic with unbound variables. The tail-recursive rule looks like this:

```
factorial2(N,Nfac,I,Temp) :-
                I =< N,
                Temp2 is Temp * I,
                I2 is I + 1,
                !,
                factorial2(N, Nfact, I2, Temp2).
```

This rule serves as a stopping condition:

```
factorial2(N, Nfac, I, Nfac) :-
                I > N.
```

To provide an initial value of 1 for I and Temp and also to simplify queries to the rule, use another predicate as a driver:

```
factorial1(N, Nfac) :-
                factorial2(N, Nfac, 1, 1).
```

Which of its three roles does the cut play in this example?

Caution in Using the Cut

You need to be cautious in using the cut because it can change the way a rule works by limiting backtracking. As an example, consider this version of append/3:

```
append([],X,X) :- !.
append([H|T1], L2, [H|T3]) :- append(L1, L2, L3).
```

This will work fine if you are forming a new list from two other lists. However, with a goal of the form

```
append(X, Y, [a,b,c]).
```

PROLOG's response will be only

```
X = []
Y = [a, b, c]
```

7.2 PROGRAMMING SUGGESTIONS

This portion of the chapter offers some suggestions to help you design and write PROLOG rules and programs. Some of these suggestions apply equally well to procedural language programming, but others are quite specific to PROLOG.

Planning a Program

You can use traditional top-down design techniques to design a PROLOG program. Implement the program modules with PROLOG rules. The advantages of modularity exist here just as in procedural programming: program clarity, simplification of tasks, potential division of labor, and independent testing of program components.

With PROLOG programs there is, however, one precaution as you create new modules: *Avoid duplicate names for rules.* This is an ever increasing hazard as programs get larger and as more people work on them.

Writing Code

The objectives in writing a PROLOG program are the same as those in any other language: (1) Make it work, and (2) make it easy to read and understand. There are several things you can do to facilitate the second of these objectives.

1. Design your rules for readability. In particular, avoid the semicolon. Instead of *or* rules, write multiple rules.

2. Format your program so that it is easy to read: Begin each new relationship on a new line. Separate different relationships with blank lines. Indent each clause in a rule on a new line. Be consistent!

3. Organize your program: Group related rules. Describe major modules with comments. When appropriate, put facts with the rules that use them.

4. Make your program as self-documenting as possible. That requires using meaningful names for rules, variables, constants, and structures. There is no excuse for using cryptic names in PROLOG programs.

5. Explain non-trivial relations in comments. For example,
   ```
   sum_to_N(N, Sum)
   %   N is an integer
   %   Sum is the sum of all integers from 0 to N
   ```

6. Provide appropriate external documentation. This includes a description of the program's purpose, its structure, the files it uses, and instructions for using the program.

8

DEVELOPING AND DEBUGGING PROGRAMS

Finding and removing errors from PROLOG programs can be difficult, especially while one is learning the language. PROLOG provides a debugging facility to help in locating errors. Also, by coding and testing programs one module (rule) at a time, programmers can minimize the possible locations for most types of errors.

This chapter begins by illustrating modular program development. A review of common errors follows. The chapter concludes with an explanation of the PROLOG debugging predicates and illustrations of their use.

8.1 MODULAR DEVELOPMENT

Listing 8.1 presents the beginnings of a program to solve a problem from Garavaglia's PROLOG text (problem 4, page 158).[1] The purpose of the program is to examine applicants for a specific job and list all of those who qualify. To qualify, an applicant must:

1. Have at least 5 years previous experience
2. Have both a bachelor's and master's degree
3. Have worked an average of at least 3 years for previous employers
4. Be willing to work overtime *or*
   Be willing to travel
5. Be in good to excellent health

---
1 Susan Garavaglia, *PROLOG: Programming Techniques and Applications*, Harper & Row, 1987.

```
%            MATCHING JOB APPLICANTS WITH JOB REQUIREMENTS
% app([Name, JobList, DegreeList, WorkOT, Travel, Health])
%      JobList     = [Employer, Years] for each employer
%      DegreeList  = List of degrees [ba, bs, ms, phd, etc.]
%      WorkOT      = willingness to work overtime  (y/n)
%      Travel      = willingness to travel (y/n)
%      Health      = state of health (poor, fair, good, v_good, excel)

app([wilson, [[white,2],[green,1],[black,7]], [bs,ms], y, n, excel]).
app([baxter, [[brown,3],[gold,2]], [bs,ms,phd], y, y, v_good]).
app([dexter, [[glass,10],[clay,8],[steel,4]], [ba], y, n, fair]).

meets_requirements(Person) :-
       app([Person, JobList, DegreeList, WorkOT, Travel, Health]),
       at_least_5_years_experience(Person, JobList),
       has_bachelors_and_masters(Person,DegreeList),
       three_plus_years_average_at_jobs(Person,JobList),
       (will_work_ot(Person, WorkOT) ; will_travel(Person, Travel)),
       good_health(Person, Health).

at_least_5_years_experience(Person, JobList) :- true.

has_bachelors_and_masters(Person, DegreeList) :- true.

three_plus_years_average_at_jobs(Person, JobList) :- true.

will_work_ot(Person,WorkOT) :- true.

will_travel(Person, Travel) :- fail.

good_health(Person, Health) :- true.
```

LISTING 8.1 Program design example

The comment lines in the figure describe the structure of the data records for the applicants. Presenting this information is a good procedure to follow in documenting all programs. The comments are a handy reference when you need to access fact lists, and, after the program is complete, they help others to understand the program. The app/6 relationships are the sample data Garavaglia provides.

The meets_requirements/1 predicate needs to succeed for those applicants who meet all of the conditions. The version you see in Listing 8.1 begins with the app/6 predicate so that successive clauses can reference all the data they need about each applicant.

The other clauses call predicates to test the five conditions listed above. Notice that these rules are incomplete. Instead of clauses to test each condition, they are defined as either true or false.

Also notice that the semicolon combines the rules to test overtime and travel; this is an exception to our suggestion that you write duplicate rules rather than writing rules with or clauses in them. We believe this is easier to read than two lengthy and quite similar rules would be. Let the question of readability be your guide.

Listing 8.1 illustrates a good way to begin a program. You can enter the predicates and facts shown there into a PROLOG database and query the meets_requirements rule. If PROLOG reports that all the persons in the app list meet the requirements, you will know that what you have entered is error free. Otherwise there are one or more errors that you will need to correct. Fortunately, any errors that do occur will be confined to these few lines of text and should be easy to find.

Once you have removed all errors, you can replace each of the rule stubs with clauses that will perform the appropriate test. As you develop each rule, test it to make sure it works before you begin working on another one. This procedure confines errors to the new program lines.

8.2 SOME COMMON ERRORS

Syntax errors occur more often than any other type. Among the more common ones are omission of a period or comma and a missing or extra parenthesis or bracket. Fortunately, the PROLOG interpreter will identify these errors before they can cause problems.

Misspellings are also common, and they are not caught by the system. They can cause PROLOG to respond with no when everything else appears to be in order.

Circular definitions that produce inadvertent recursion are another hazard to avoid. Here is an example:

```
parent(X,Y) :- child(Y,X).
child(X,Y) :- parent(Y,X).
```

While you are not likely to write a pair of definitions like this at one sitting, you might enter them into your database on different days, especially if your program is large. Even more likely is a longer chain of circular definitions. Be alert for them.

Referring to a rule with an incorrect number of arguments produces an elusive error. For example, this reference to the app/6 fact list in Listing 8.1 is incorrect:

```
app([Person, JobList, _, _, _])
```

Were this reference used as a condition in a rule, it would always evaluate to false because the arity of app is six rather than five.

Incorrect referencing of the list notation can cause problems, too. Referencing the app/6 predicate in this way would prevent the correct instantiation:

```
app([Person, [JobList], _, _, _, _])
```

The brackets around JobList are the error.

8.3 PROLOG'S DEBUGGING PREDICATES

PROLOG provides standard predicates that allow you to follow the execution of a program. *Trace* is a predicate that tells PROLOG to report this information. Listing 8.2 contains an example of a small database and the trace of a query to one of its rules. These are the different types of information that the trace provides:

CALL reports PROLOG's first attempt to satisfy a goal.

EXIT reports that a goal is satisfied.

REDO reports any attempt after the first to satisfy a goal.

FAIL reports the failure of a goal.

Trace takes no arguments. Entering "trace." turns the trace facility on. Entering "notrace." turns it off. You may also turn tracing on and off from the pull-down Debug menu. To move from one trace statement to the next, tap the letter c.

In Listing 8.2, the trace begins by reporting the call, (0) CALL, to the head of the rule with Day instantiated to th and the variable Sandwich indicated by _0038. (PROLOG keeps track of its internal operations with variable names beginning with the underscore and followed by a number.) To continue, the user enters the letter c following the trace prompt, >.

The next call, (1) CALL, is the condition sandwich(th, _0038). When PROLOG finds a sandwich/2 fact with th as the first argument, it instantiates _0038 to peanut_butter_and_jelly and reports the success of the goal in the (1) EXIT statement. (0) EXIT reports success of the main goal. Next the system interrupts the trace to provide its usual success statement.

After its first success, PROLOG responds to the semicolon and continues looking for other ways to satisfy the goal. (0) REDO begins a sequence just like the one that began with (1) CALL. After the second success, PROLOG can find no more ways to satisfy the goal and so the trace ends.

Listing 8.3 shows you the difference between a trace of a rule that works and a version of the rule with an error in it. The only difference between the two versions is the set of list brackets around the JobList variable in the add_years_worked/2 clause.

The first trace shows how PROLOG works through the recursive calls, totals the years worked, and determines that they amount to at least five. The

8.3 PROLOG'S DEBUGGING PREDICATES

```
todays_sandwich(Day, Sandwich) :- sandwich(Day, Sandwich).

sandwich(m, hamburger).
sandwich(tu, blt).
sandwich(w, grilled_cheese).
sandwich(th, peanut_butter_and_jelly).
sandwich(f, fish).
sandwich(th, butter_and_honey).
```

(Indented statements appear in the debugging window.)

```
?- trace.
yes

?- todays_sandwich(th, Sandwich).
          (0)   CALL: todays_sandwich(th, _0038) ? > c

          (1)   CALL: sandwich(th, _0038) ? > c

          (1)   EXIT(N): sandwich(th,peanut_butter_and_jelly)
          (0)   EXIT(N): todays_sandwich(th,peanut_butter_and_jelly)
     Type any key to continue.

Sandwich = peanut_butter_and_jelly ->;

          (0)   REDO: todays_sandwich(th,peanut_butter_and_jelly) ? > c

          (1)   REDO: sandwich(peanut_butter_and_jelly) ? > c

          (1)   EXIT(D): sandwich(th, butter_and_honey)
          (0)   EXIT(D): todays_sandwich(th, butter_and_honey)
     Type any key to continue.

Sandwich = butter_and_honey ->;

     Type any key to continue.

no
?-
```

LISTING 8.2 An example of a trace

second trace shows you that PROLOG attempts to perform arithmetic with an entire list rather than using the number in the list. Once you see what is happening, it is a simple matter to correct the problem.

A common problem users encounter with trace is the vast amount of information it reports. To avoid being inundated with page after page of trace

CHAPTER 8 DEVELOPING AND DEBUGGING PROGRAMS

```
at_least_5_years_experience(Person, JobList) :-
      add_years_worked(JobList, Years_worked),
      Years_worked >= 5.

add_years_worked([], 0) :- !.
add_years_worked([[H,Yr|T] | Tail], Years) :-
      add_years_worked(Tail, Years2),
      Years is Yr + Years2.
```

Trace exerpt with rules as shown above

```
?- at_least_5_years_experience(billings, [[bird, 3], [deere, 7]]).
(0)    CALL: at_least_5_years_experience(billings, [[bird,3],[deere,7]]) ? > c
(1)    CALL: add_years_worked([[bird, 3], [deere, 7]], _16E8) ? > c
(2)    CALL: add_years_worked([[deere, 7]], _17A4) ? > c
(3)    CALL: add_years_worked([], _186C) ? > c
(4)    CALL: ! ? ,> c

(4)    EXIT(D): !
(3)    EXIT(D): add_years_worked([], 0)
(5)    CALL: (3) _17A4 is 7 + 0 ? > c

(5)    EXIT(D): 7 is 7 + 0
(2)    EXIT(D): add_years_worked([deere, 7],7)

(6)    CALL: _16E8 is 3 + 7 ? > c

(6)    EXIT(D): 10 is 3 + 7
(1)    EXIT(D): add_years_worked([[bird, 3], [deere, 7]], 10)
(7)    CALL: 10 >= 5 ? > c

(7)    EXIT(D): 10 >= 5
(0)    EXIT(D): at_least_5_years_experience(billings, [[bird, 3], [deere, 7]])
Type any key to continue.
yes
```

Trace exerpt with following version of experience rule

```
at_least_5_years_experience(Person, JobList) :-
      add_years_worked([JobList], Years_worked),
      Years_worked >= 5.

?- at_least_5_years_experience(billings, [[bird,3], [deere, 7]]).
(0)    CALL: at_least_5_years_experience(billings, [[bird,3],[deere,7]]) ? > c
(1)    CALL: add_years_worked([[[bird,3], [deere,7]]],_1740) ? > c
(2)    CALL: add_years_worked([],_1804) ? > c
(3)    CALL: ! ? > c
```

LISTING 8.3 (Continued next page)

```
(3)    EXIT(D):  !
(2)    EXIT(D): add_years_worked([], 0)
(2)    CALL: _1740 is [deere,7] + 0 ? > c

(4)    EXIT(D): err is [deere,7] + 0
(1)    EXIT(D): add_years_worked([[bird,3],[deere,7]]],err)
(5)    CALL: err >= 5 ? > c

(5)    FAIL: err >= 5
(0)    FAIL: at_least_5_years_experience(billings, [[bird,3], [deere,7]])
Type any key to continue.
no
```

LISTING 8.3 Trace of correct and incorrect rules (continued)

information, you can use another of PROLOG's tracing predicates, spy. *Spy* provides the same information as trace except that it reports it only for a single predicate.

To set a spy point for a specific predicate, say the ancestor/2 rules, enter

```
spy ancestor.
```

To turn it off for the same rule set, enter

```
nospy ancestor.
```

You may turn spy on for as many predicates as you like.

You may also turn spy on and off in the Debug menu. Pull down the menu and select the Spy option from the Debug menu, move the cursor to the predicate that is to have the spy point set or removed and press the space bar. To remove all spy points, enter

```
resetspy.
```

at the applications window prompt.

To use a spy point, turn tracing on and enter a goal. Then, instead of pressing c to continue to the next step, press l and execution will "leap" to the first spy point. Pressing l again will take you to the next spy point step.

There are many other options you may use while in the Debug window. Figure 8.1 lists them with a brief explanation of each.

If, while using the debugger, you want to view the applications window, press the space bar. Pressing the space bar again toggles you back to the Debug window.

COMMAND	EXPLANATION
a	Abort. Aborts program execution, turns off the debugger, and returns to the interpreter prompt.
b	Break. Interrupts the debugging procedure without terminating the program execution. The interpreter prompt indicates the number of breaks in effect. (??- indicates 2 breaks) Ctrl-Z causes execution and debugging to resume.
c	Creep. Causes the debugger to advance to the next step. Note: You can also creep by pressing the Enter key.
d	Display goal. Displays the current goal.
e	Exit. Exits the interpreter.
f	Fail. Causes the debugger to continue to the next FAIL step.
h	Help. Displays the Debug help screen (which explains these commands). Tap Esc to return to the Debug window
l	Leap. Causes the Debugger to leap from one spy point to the next.
n	Nodebug. Turns the debugger off.
q	Quasi skip. Skips to the exit or fail step of the current goal unless there is spy point set in the goal; execution stops at the spy point in the goal if one is set
s	Skip. Skips to the exit or fail step of the current goal. This command is acceptable only at a call or redo step. This command can also be entered with the Esc key.
w	Write goal. Writes the current goal in the Debug window.
x	Back to choice point. Causes the debugger to continue failing until a call or exit step is reached. Can only be used at a fail or redo step.
z	Zip. Skips to the EXIT or FAIL step of a goal regardless of spy points that may be set. No information on backtracking is maintained. Use only from a CALL or REDO.
@	Accept goal. Allows you to call a PROLOG goal. Upon completion of the goal, the trace continues.
;	Redo. Causes the Debugger to proceed to the redo step of the current goal. Can only be used at an exit port.
space	Toggles between the Debugger window and the applications window.

FIGURE 8.1 Arity Prolog's debugging commands

9
A FEW ARITY PROLOG EXTRAS

In this chapter we present a few of the special features available to users of Arity Prolog. Each feature will be discussed briefly and will be followed by a short example. A large program that incorporates these features is included at the end of the chapter.

9.1 WINDOWS

Arity Prolog predicates that allow the user to create, maintain, and use windows include those in Figure 9.1. In the standard Arity Prolog syntax, a plus sign (+) indicates that the argument must be instantiated and a minus (-) means that it must be uninstantiated. Arguments preceded with a question mark (?) may be either instantiated or uninstantiated.

Define_window/5 defines a new window. The first argument names the window while the second argument, if present, contains text enclosed in single quotes, which will be displayed in the top-left-hand side of the window. The (ULR, ULC) pair indicate the Row and Column position of the upper-left-hand corner of the window while (LRR, LRC) gives the position of the lower-right-hand corner.

The final attribute pair, (Window_attr, Border_attr) specifies the display attributes of the window and its border. These attributes follow the standard IBM PC conventions for color, bold, and reverse video. A positive border_attr will cause a single-line border to be displayed; a negative number indicates a double-line border and zero is used to indicate that no border should be displayed.

```
define_window(+Name,?Label,?(ULR,ULC),?(LRR,LRC),?(Window_attr,Border_attr))

window_info(?Name,?Label,?(ULR,ULC),?(LRR,LRC),?(Window_attr,Border_attr))

current_window(-Old,?New)

hide_window(-Current,+New)

what_windows(-Name)

resize_window(+Rows,+Columns)

move_window(+Rows,Columns)

relabel_window(+Label)

recolor_window(+Window_attr,+Border_attr)

delete_window(+Name)
```

FIGURE 9.1 Predicates for windows

Window_info/5 is used to determine attributes of the current window. This might be used prior to changing the position or size of the window or changing its attributes.

PROLOG output always goes to the currently active window. Define_window/5 defines a window but it does not display or activate the window. Activation (and display) are controlled by current_window/2 and hide_window/2. Current_window/2 returns the name of the current window as Old and then actives the new window, New. Old is left on the screen (but may be partially or completely covered by New). Hide_window/2 does the same thing as current_window/2 except that Old is hidden (but not deleted).

Resize_window/2 and move_window/2 change the size of or move the current window by Rows rows and Columns columns. Negative numbers may be used to decrease the size of the window or to move it to the left or toward the top. Relabel_window/1 changes the label of the current window and recolor_window/2 changes its attributes.

What_windows/1 will return the names of all current windows (through backtracking) and can be used to be determine if a particular window exists. Finally, delete_window/1 removes the definition of a window.

Listing 9.1 illustrates the use of several of the windows predicates and the resulting windows are in Figure 9.2 (the sample screens were captured at each get0/1).

```
/* sample windows program */
windows:-
    cls,
    define_window(window1,'This is window one label',(2,5),(12,55),(1,1)),
    define_window(window2,'This is window two label (Notice the double lines)',
              (11,10),(17,65),(2,-2)),
    define_window(window3,'This is window three label',(19,10),(21,60),(4,6)),
    current_window(Old,window1),
    write(old_window=Old),
    nl,
    write('This is a long line of text written after the activation of window number
1. As you can see, the text wraps inside the window. (But without regard to word
boundaries)'),
    get0(X),
    get0(A),
    current_window(Old2,window2),
    write(' Now we are writing in window number two!'),
    nl,nl,nl,
    write('This is still window number two.'),
    get0(Y),
    current_window(Old3,window3),
    write('Small windows like this are good for messages!'),
    get0(Z),
    hide_window(window3,window1),
    cls,
    write('This is what things look like after hiding window three and reactivating
window one. Notice that the clear screen command only cleared the current window!'),
    get0(XX).

delete_windows:-
    delete_window(window1),
    delete_window(window2),
    delete_window(window3).
```

LISTING 9.1

Some windows are created for a brief communication with the user and then deleted. The term "pop-up" window has often been used to describe this type of activity. Arity Prolog supports the concept of pop-up windows with a predicate called create_popup/4. The attributes of create_popup/4 are the same as the first four attributes of create_window/5; there is no Name attribute.

A pop-up window becomes the current window as soon as it is created; you do not need to use (in fact, cannot use) current_window/2 or hide_window/2. A pop-up window remains current until the predicate, exit_popup/0 is executed. You may not switch to another window while a popup is active.

80   CHAPTER 9   A FEW ARITY PROLOG EXTRAS

```
┌ M A I N ═══════════════════════════════════════════════════
│  ┌This is window one label─────────────────┐
│  │ old_window = main                       │
│  │ This is a long line of text written after the act
│  │ ivation of window number 1.  As you can see, the
│  │ text wraps inside the window. (But without regard
│  │  to word boundaries)                    │
│  │                                         │
│  └─────────────────────────────────────────┘
└ ═══════════════════════════════════════════════════════════


┌ M A I N ═══════════════════════════════════════════════════
│  ┌This is window one label─────────────────┐
│  │ old_window = main                       │
│  │ This is a long line of text written after the act
│  │ ivation of window number 1.  As you can see, the
│  │ text wraps inside the window. (But without regard
│  │  to word boundaries)                    │
│  │      ┌This is window two label (Notice the double lines)═══┐
│  │      │ Now we are writing in window number two!            │
│  └──────│                                                     │
│         │ This is still window number two.                    │
│         │                                                     │
│         └─────────────────────────────────────────────────────┘
└ ═══════════════════════════════════════════════════════════


┌ M A I N ═══════════════════════════════════════════════════
│  ┌This is window one label─────────────────┐
│  │ old_window = main                       │
│  │ This is a long line of text written after the act
│  │ ivation of window number 1.  As you can see, the
│  │ text wraps inside the window. (But without regard
│  │  to word boundaries)                    │
│  │      ┌This is window two label (Notice the double lines)═══┐
│  │      │ Now we are writing in window number two!            │
│  └──────│                                                     │
│         │ This is still window number two.                    │
│         │                                                     │
│         │  ┌This is window three label──────────────┐         │
│         │  │ Small windows like this are good for messages! │
│         │  └────────────────────────────────────────┘         │
└ ═══════════════════════════════════════════════════════════


┌ M A I N ═══════════════════════════════════════════════════
│  ┌This is window one label─────────────────┐
│  │ This is what things look like after hiding window
│  │  three and reactivating window one.  Notice that
│  │  the clear screen command only cleared the current
│  │  window!                                │
│  │                                         │
│  │                                         ines)═══┐
│  │                                                 │
│  │         This is still window number two.        │
│  │                                                 │
│  └─────────────────────────────────────────────────┘
└ ═══════════════════════════════════════════════════════════
```

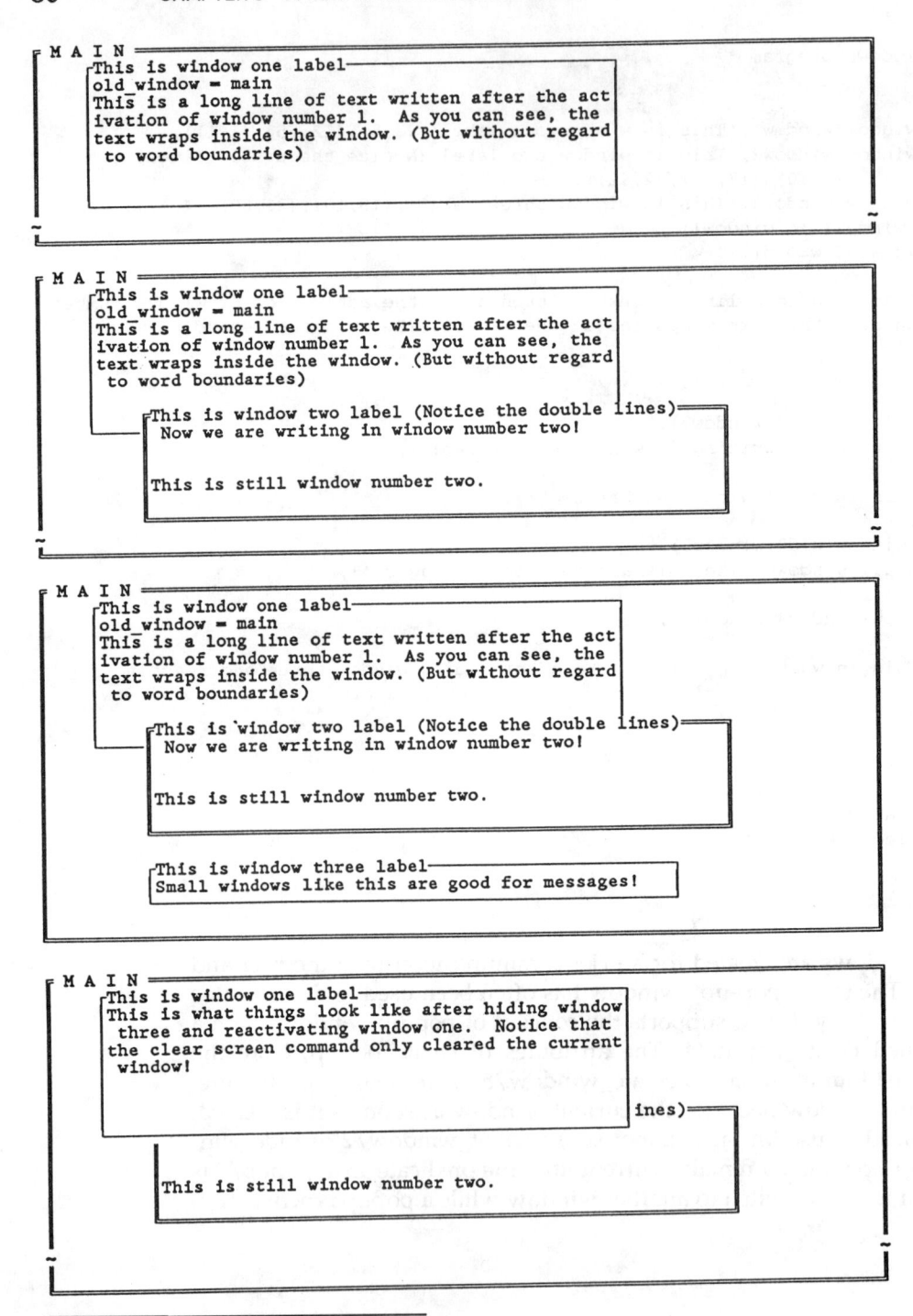

FIGURE 9.2 Some sample programs

```
mouse/0        /*   reset mouse values   */

show_mouse_cursor/0
            /*   shows the position of the mouse cursor on the screen   */

hide_mouse_cursor/0

set_mouse_position(+Row,+Column)
            /*   move the mouse cursor to Row and Col of the screen   */

get_mouse_position(-Row,-Column,State)
            /*   returns the current Row and Column position of the mouse.  If State
                 = 0, no mouse button is pressed.  State = 1 when the left button is
                 pressed and state = 2 when the right button is pressed.  State = 3
                 means that both buttons are pressed (Note, three button mice like
                 the Logitech Mouse return 4 when the middle button is pressed)   */
```

FIGURE 9.3 Some mouse predicates

9.2 MOUSE RELATED THINGS

Arity Prolog comes with a special library of predicates called the *bonus.lib*.[1] Included in this library is a list of predicates that allow a PROLOG program to access information from a Microsoft (or compatible) Mouse. Among the mouse predicates found in the library are those shown in Figure 9.3.

The program in Listing 9.2 uses get_mouse_position/3 to determine information about the mouse and then displays the information on the bottom of the screen. Positioning is done with another Arity predicate, tmove/2, which positions the text cursor at the specified row and column.

We will return to a more useful mouse example after discussing Arity's database functions and menu capabilities.

9.3 DATABASE MANAGEMENT

You are already acquainted with several standard database predicates used to manipulate PROLOG clauses including: clause/2, asserta/1, assertz/1, retract/1, and abolish/1. In addition to these common predicates, Arity Prolog has a number of predicates that facilitate storage, manipulation, and access of data (as opposed to clauses).

---
1 A VERY IMPORTANT NOTE: In order to use any of the bonus library predicates, the library must be compiled and linked to the Arity interpreter. Instructions on how to do this are included in the Arity documentation related to the *bonus.lib* library. The sample program shown below will not work unless this has been done!

CHAPTER 9 A FEW ARITY PROLOG EXTRAS

```
/* mouse check */
   mouse_loop:-
        repeat,
        get_mouse_position(X,Y,Z),
        check_mouse(X,Y,Z).
   check_mouse(_,_,3):-
        !.
   check_mouse(X,Y,Z):-
        tmove(20,5),
        write(X),
        write(' '),
        write(Y),
        write(' '),
        write(Z),
        write('      '),
        fail.

   ck:-get_mouse_position(X,Y,Z),
        write(X),
        write(' '),
        write(Y),
        write(' '),
        write(Z).
```

LISTING 9.2

Each set of terms stored in the database has a *key*. The key of a clause stored in the database is it's predicate name and arity. Other kinds of data have keys specified by the programmer. Each item stored in the database is assigned a unique reference number by Arity Prolog. All like terms are stored as a circular linked list. The key points to the first term in the list and each term is linked to the next. The last term in the list is linked back to the key.

Some of Arity's database-management predicates are described in Figure 9.4. The use of some of them is illustrated in the simple example in Listing 9.3. Notice that *item(forth)* is at the beginning of the list because it was saved with recorda/3. Notice also that *item(fifth)* follows *item(second)* because it was stored with record_after/3 using the reference number of *item(second)*.

We will illustrate more of the database-management predicates in an example as soon as we discuss Arity's menu capabilities. All of the database-management predicates are available for use at any time. Note, also, that Arity's Dialog Box feature makes extensive use of the database-management predicates. (Several examples of Dialog Boxes are found in the object-oriented design program. A detailed discussion of Dialog Boxes is beyond the scope of this chapter; refer to the Arity Prolog reference manual for more information.)

```
recorda(+Key,+Term,-Ref)
     /* stores 'Term' at the beginning of the list for 'Key'.  Prolog returns
        reference number of this term as 'Ref'*/
recordz(+Key,+Term,-Ref)
     /* same as recorda/3 except that Term is placed at the end of the
        list for 'Key' */
record_after(+Ref,+Term,-NewRef)
     /* 'Term' is stored after the term with reference number 'Ref' */
recorded(+Key,?Term,-Ref)
     /* searches the database for 'Term' stored under 'Key' and returns the Term
        and its Ref number.  Can be used to find all terms associated with a key
        through backtracking */
instance(+Ref,-Term)
     /* returns the 'Term' with reference number 'Ref') */
key(+Key,-Ref)1
     /* returns the reference number, 'Ref', for the first item with key, 'Key' */
nref(+Ref,-Next)
     /* returns the 'Next' reference number in the change */
pref(+Ref,-Prev)
     /* returns the reference number of the Previous term in the chain */
replace(+Ref,+Term)
     /* replace the term with reference number 'Ref' with 'Term'.  This is similar
        to a retract followed by an assert */
erase(+Ref)
     /* erase the term with reference number 'Ref' */
eraseall(+Key)
     /* erase all terms stored under 'Key' */
```

FIGURE 9.4 Database-management predicates

9.4 MENUS

Arity Prolog has a facility that makes it easy to design custom pull-down menus. This facility requires that you first define a menu and then send it messages asking it to become active (display itself and wait for the user to make a selection).

Menu definitions must be stored in a file which is consulted while the program is running. The format of a menu definition file is

```
/* Arity database predicate example */
   dbtest:-
           recordz(test,item(first),Ref1),
           recordz(test,item(second),Ref2),
           recordz(test,item(third),Ref3),
           recorda(test,item(forth),Ref4),
           record_after(Ref2,item(fifth),_),
           list_recorded.

   list_recorded:-
           recorded(test,X,_),
           nl,
           write(X),
           fail.
   list_recorded.

?- dbtest.

item(forth)
item(first)
item(second)
item(fifth)
item(third)
yes
```

LISTING 9.3

```
       begin_menu(Name,Length,colors((TNormal,TReverse),
             (PNormal,PReverse),(GNormal,GReverse),(Accel,Border)))

             /* menu items go here */

       end_menu(Name)
```

Name is an atom that identifies this menu. Length is the total length of the menu bar, in characters. Length must be long enough to hold all of the menu choices and must fit in the current window when the menu is activated.

The colors/4 structure contains colors for various screen attributes used in the menu. The TNormal/TReverse pair refers to the top-level items, the entries on the menu bar itself. TNormal is used when an item isn't selected and TReverse is the attribute used when the cursor is on an item. PNormal and PReverse serve the same function for pull-down menu items. GNormal/GReverse are used with items that have been "grayed" or inactivated. Accel is used to indicate an accelerator key, a key that can be used to quickly select a menu item. Finally, Border defines the border around the menu.

Menu items may take one of these three forms:

```
item(Label,[PDDef1,PDDef2...])
              /* Label is the name of the menu item that will be displayed
                 on the menu bar. PDDef1, PDDef2, etc. are pull-down menu
                 definitions */

item(Label,ReturnVal)
              /* ReturnVal is a value that will be returned when the menu item is
                 selected */

item(Label,ReturnVal,grayed)   /* the item will initially be grayed */
```

Labels are strings and must be enclosed in dollar signs ($). A title may be used to indicate an accelerator key (e.g., `$~Window$` is a valid label for a menu item called "window," which can be activated with the W key).

Pull-down menu definitions (`PDDef1`, etc.) are exactly the same as regular items except that they are in a list associated with the top-level item. Pull-down menus may contain a special item called *break*, which will cause a horizontal line to be drawn in the menu.

Consider the menu definition in Listing 9.4. When added to a program, it will produce menus like those shown in Figure 9.5. A PROLOG program that uses the menu definition to draw these menus and the output after selecting several menu items is shown in Listing 9.5.

```
/*  menus for object system */

begin_menu(objectmenu,70,colors((113,63),(113,63),(80,81),(117,117))).
item($~Objects$,[item($~Draw objects$,draw),
     item($~Redraw all objects$,redraw),
     break,
     item($~Erase all objects$,delete),
     break,
     item($~Change size of object$,resize),
     item($~Move object$,move)]).
item($~Select$,[item($with ~Mouse$,mouse),item($from a ~List...$,list)]).
item($~Attributes$,[item($Edit object attributes...$,attributes)]).
item($~HideMenu$,[item($Temporarily hide the menu$,hide)]).
item($~Process$,[item($~Transform definitions$,transform),
     item($~Data Entry$,dataentry),
     item($Data ~Edit$,dataedit),
     item($Expand ~Sample Objects$,realize)]).
item($~End$,[item($End program$,end),
     item($Issue a ~Break command$,break),
     item($~Save current database$,save),
     item($~Reload saved database$,reload)]).
end_menu(objectmenu).
```

LISTING 9.4

CHAPTER 9 A FEW ARITY PROLOG EXTRAS

```
  Objects  Select  Attributes  HideMenu  Process  End
  ┌─────────────────────────┐
  │ Redraw all objects      │
  │ Erase all objects       │
  │ Change size of object   │
  │ Move object             │
  └─────────────────────────┘


  Objects  Select  Attributes  HideMenu  Process  End
                                         ┌──────────────────────┐
                                         │ Data Entry           │
                                         │ Data Edit            │
                                         │ Expand Sample Objects│
                                         └──────────────────────┘
```

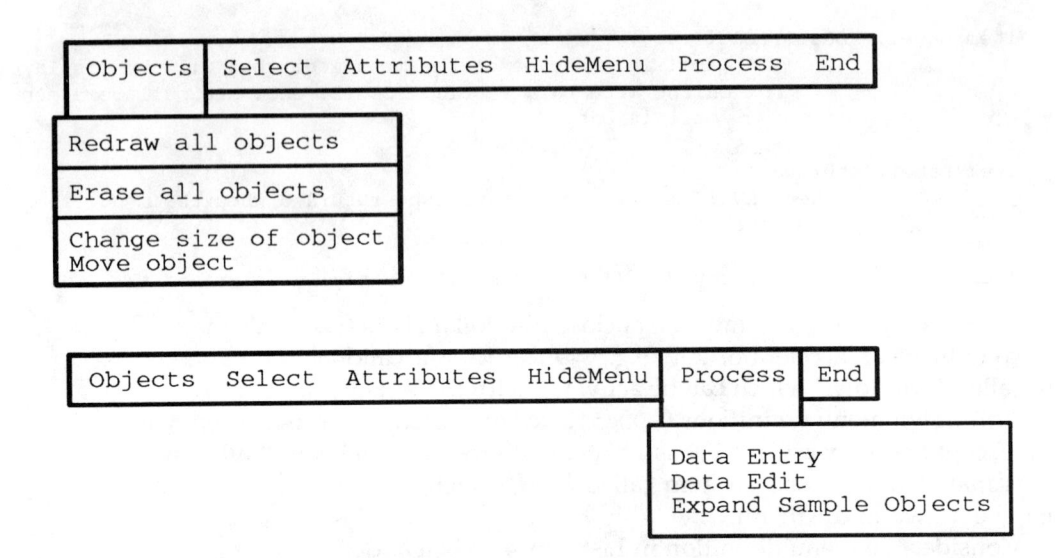

FIGURE 9.5

```
test:-
        [-'menu.def'],    /* definition must be loaded by consultation */
        cls,
        tmove(18,0),
        repeat,
        send_menu_msg(activate(objectmenu,(1,1)),ReturnVal),
        write(return_value = ReturnVal),
        nl,
        ReturnVal == end.



return_value = draw
return_value = attributes
return_value = dataentry
return_value = realize
return_value = end
```

LISTING 9.5

As you can see from this example, the command that activates the menu is called send_menu_msg/2. The first argument says to display and activate the menu called objectmenu. The (1,1) indicates the position of the upper-left-hand corner of the menu *in the current window*. The general format of this predicate is

```
send_menu_msg(activate(+MenuName,(+Row,+Col)),-ReturnVal)
```

If you wish to display the menu without accepting input, use the menu message *draw*.

```
send_menu_msg(draw(+MenuName,(+Row,+Col)),true).
```

Once drawn, the window will stay on the screen until one of the following happens: the program ends, the window containing the menu is closed, a clear-screen command is issued, or enough text is written to cause the window to scroll off the screen. Displaying the menu inside a pop-up window is an easy way to ensure that the menu is removed when no longer needed.

When the menu is displayed, you may move from one menu choice to another with the right and left arrow keys. The down arrow key is used to open a pull-down menu. Once opened, the up and down arrow keys move you though the pull-down menu while the right and left arrow keys move from one pull-down to another. To close a pull-down menu, press escape. Pressing escape from the top level of a menu sends a return value of "cancel."

Please note that Arity Prolog has additional predicates for changing menu attributes and for checking and changing the "grayed" status of menu items. Check the reference manual for the exact syntax.

9.5 AN EXAMPLE

We end this chapter with a sample program that allows you to draw windows on the screen with the mouse. Once drawn, the windows can be moved, resized, or deleted. You may also use the mouse to select the active window. The current active window is indicated with a double border, and all other windows have a single border. Data on the windows is managed with Arity's special database-management functions, and menus are used to select the desired action.

The main/0 predicate in Listing 9.6 loads the menu definitions from a file called *obj-boxes.ari* and then defines a main window (`object`) and a message window (`msg`). Window definitions are stored in the database as windows/8 structures under the key, object. Initialize_key/1 removes any entries leftover from a previous execution.

Main/0 calls main_loop/0 which uses a repeat loop to display the menu in a pop-up window and call menu/1 with the menu selection. This loop continues until the End program option is selected from the menu. End program has a `ReturnVal`, X in this case, of `end`.

Each menu/1 clause contains a menu `ReturnVal` as its single argument. As you can see from the code in Listing 9.7, most menu/1 clauses simply call another clause that will perform the intended action. The final menu/1 clause catches unimplemented menu choices and displays a pop-up message window.

CHAPTER 9 A FEW ARITY PROLOG EXTRAS

```
main:-
    [-'obj-boxs.ari'],
    define_window(object,_,(0,0),(23,79),(2,0)),
    define_window(msg,_,(24,1),(24,78),(32,0)),
    current_window(_,object),
    abolish(current/1),
    initialize_key(object),
    asserta(current(object)),
    recorda(object,windows(object,0,0,23,79,_,2,0),_),
    cls,
    main_loop.

main_loop:-
    repeat,
        create_popup('Object Menu',(0,2),(9,77),(11,11)),
    send_menu_msg(activate(objectmenu,(0,1)),X),
    exit_popup,
    menu(X),
    X == end.
```

LISTING 9.6

```
menu(draw):-                        % Build windows based on mouse click
    clear_mouse,                    %   left click marks upper left corner
    set_mouse_position(10,1)        %   right click marks lower right corner */
    show_mouse_cursor,
    repeat,
    build_window(B1,B2),
    (B1 =:= 4 ; B2 =:= 4),
    hide_mouse_cursor,
    current_window(Window,msg),     % remove the line 25 msg
    cls,
    current_window(_,Window),
    !.

menu(redraw):-
    redraw,
    !.

menu(resize):-
    resize_object,
    !.

menu(move):-
    move_object,
    !.
```

LISTING 9.7   (Continued next page)

9.5 AN EXAMPLE

```
menu(mouse):-
    clear_mouse,
    show_mouse_cursor,
    current_window(Old,msg),
    write($Point to object, press right and left buttons at the same time to select$),
    current_window(_,Old),
    cw,
    hide_mouse_cursor,
    current_window(Current,msg),
    cls,
    current_window(_,Current),
    !.

menu(delete):-
    dw,
    define_window(object,_,(0,0),(23,79),(2,0)),
    define_window(msg,_,(24,1),(24,78),(32,0)),
    current_window(_,object),
    recorda(object,windows(object,0,0,23,79,_,2,0),_),
    !.

menu(hide):-
    current_window(Old,msg),
    write($Press any mouse button to redisplay the menu$),
    current_window(_,Old),
    repeat,
    get_mouse_position(_,_,Button),
    Button =\= 0,
    current_window(Current,msg),
    cls,
    current_window(_,Current),
    !.

menu(end):-
    dw,
    !.

menu(_):-
    create_popup(_,(10,17),(13,63),(79,192)),
    cls,
    write($That function hasn't been implemented yet.$),
    nl,
    write($      Press return to continue$),
    read_line(0,X),
    exit_popup.
```

LISTING 9.7 (Continued)

CHAPTER 9 A FEW ARITY PROLOG EXTRAS

We will not go through all of this program here but will look at a few examples. First, consider the menu(draw) clause shown in Listing 9.7. This predicate calls clear_mouse/0 to reset the mouse, sets the mouse cursor at an arbitrary position, and displays it. It then enters a repeat loop that will continue until a window has been defined or the user aborts the procedure. The actual window creation is controlled by build_window/2.

Build_window/2 in Listing 9.8 activates the message window and displays instructions. It then reactivates the old window and calls get_top/3 which returns the position of the upper-left-corner of the new window. Next, build_temp/3 is used to create a temporary window (one without a border) that will change in size until the user selects the position of the lower-right-hand corner (determined by get_bottom/3). Finally, get_remaining_information/6 uses a pop-up window to get the name and attributes of the window.

```
build_window(B1,B2):-
    current_window(XOld,msg),
    cls,
    write($Point to upper left, press LEFT button or press the MIDDLE button to
stop$),
    current_window(_,XOld),
    get_top(TR,TC,B1),
    build_temp(TR,TC,B1),
    current_window(YOld,msg),
    cls,
    write($Point to lower right, press RIGHT button or press MIDDLE button to stop$),
    current_window(_,YOld),
    get_bottom(BR,BC,B1,B2),
    get_remaining_information(B1,B2,Name,Title,Attrib1,Attrib2),
    define_new_window(B1,B2,TR,TC,BR,BC,Name,Title,Attrib1,Attrib2),
    !.

get_bottom(BR,BC,B1,B2):-
    B1 =\= 4,
    get_mouse(BR,BC,2,B2),
    !.

get_bottom(_,_,4,4):-
    !.

get_mouse(X,Y,Wanted,Found):-
    repeat,
    get_mouse_position(X,Y,Found),
    resize(X,Y,Wanted,Found), /* this code is shown in the last section */
    AbsWanted is abs(Wanted),
    check_button(AbsWanted,Found),!.
```

LISTING 9.8 (Continued next page)

9.5 AN EXAMPLE

```
get_remaining_information(B1,B2,Name,Name,Attrib,Attrib):-
    B1 =\= 4,
    B2 =\= 4,
    create_popup(_,(1,5),(6,75),(27,-27)),
    repeat,
    cls,
    write('Please enter a one word name of this object: '),
    read_line(0,StrName),
    StrName \= $$,
    string_term(StrName,Name),
    /* test for and existing window with this name */
    ifthen(window_info(Name,_,(_,_),(_,_),(_,_)),name_error),
    write('Please enter an attribute number for the background/text: '),
    read_string(5,SX),
    int_text(TAttrib,SX),
    ifthenelse(TAttrib > 128, Attrib is TAttrib - 128, Attrib is TAttrib),
    !,
    exit_popup.

get_remaining_information(B1,B2,Name,Name,Attrib,Boarder).

get_top(TR,TC,B1):-
    get_mouse(TR,TC,1,B1),
    !.
build_temp(TR,TC,B1):-
    B1 =\= 4,
    TBR is TR  + 2,
    TBC is TC + 2,
    define_window(temp,'',(TR,TC),(TBR,TBC),(80,0)),
    current_window(_,temp),
    asserta(tempsize(TR,TC,TBR,TBC)).

build_temp(_,_,_):-
    current(Window),
    current_window(_,Window),
    delete_window(temp),
    abolish(tempsize/4),
    fail.

build_temp(_,_,4).

define_new_window(B1,B2,TR,TC,BR,BC,Name,Title,Attrib1,Attrib2):-
    B1 =\= 4,
    B2 =\= 4,
    define_window(Name,Title,(TR,TC),(BR,BC),(Attrib1,Attrib2)),
    recordz(object,windows(Name,TR,TC,BR,BC,Title,Attrib1,Attrib2),_),
    X is BR - 1,
    Y is BC - 1,
    set_mouse_position(X,Y),
    retract(current(OldWindow)),
```

LISTING 9.8 (Continued next page)

CHAPTER 9 A FEW ARITY PROLOG EXTRAS

```
        asserta(current(Name)),
        recorda(Name,$$,_),
        recordz(keys,key(Name,$undefined$),_),
        current_window(_,OldWindow),
        activate_window(Name),
        !.

define_new_window(B1,B2,TR,TC,BR,BC,Name,Title,Attrib1,Attrib2).
```

LISTING 9.8   (Continued)

The remaining code for the program is in Listing 9.9. We suggest that you load the code for this example and explore the possibilities for yourself.

```
activate_window(Window):-
    window_info(Name,_,(_,_),(_,_),(OldAttrib,OldBorder)),
    ChgBorder is abs(OldBorder),
    recolor_window(OldAttrib,ChgBorder),
    /* change border to single line and redraw objects & attributes */
    current_window(_,Window),
    window_info(_,_,(_,_),(_,_),(NewAttrib,NewBorder)),
    ChgNewBorder is -1 * abs(NewBorder),
    recolor_window(NewAttrib,ChgNewBorder).

auto_resize(Difference):-
    resize_window(0,Difference),
    window_info(Name,_,(TR,TC),(BR,BC),(_,_)),
    recorded(object,windows(Name,_,_,_,_,T1,T2,T3),Ref),
    replace(Ref,windows(Name,TR,TC,BR,BC,T1,T2,T3)).


check_button(X,X).

check_button(_,4).

/* disable this for compiled version */
check_button(_,7):-break.

check_object_size(Window,Size):-
    attrib_length(Largest),
    window_info(_,_,(TR,TC),(BR,BC),(_,_)),
    Difference is Largest - (BC - TC - 5),
    ifthen(Difference > 0, auto_resize(Difference)),
    ifthenelse(Difference > 0, Size is Largest + 5, Size is BC - TC).
```

LISTING 9.9   (Continued next page)

9.5 AN EXAMPLE

```
check_position(X,Y,_):-
    /* check to see that the current mouse position is
        inside an existing window */
    recorded(object,windows(Window,TR,TC,BR,BC,_,_,_),_),
    TR =< X,
    X =< BR,
    TC =< Y,
    Y =< BC,
    retract(current(_)),
    asserta(current(Window)),
    fail.

check_position(_,_,Window):-
    current(Window).

clear_mouse:-
    /* clear all mouse data, just to be safe */
    mouse_press(0,_,_,_,_),
    mouse_press(1,_,_,_,_),
    mouse_release(0,_,_,_,_),
    mouse_release(1,_,_,_,_).


cw:-
    /* this predicate waits until both the right and left mouse
       buttons are pushed and then determines which window
       to activate. The default window (object) is ignored */
    show_mouse_cursor,
    abolish(current/1),
    asserta(current(object)),
    repeat,
    get_mouse_position(X,Y,Pos),
    check_button(3,Pos),
    check_position(X,Y,Window),
    Window \= object,
    activate_window(Window),
        !.


dw:-
    recorded(object,windows(X,_,_,_,_,_,_,_),Ref),
    erase(Ref),
    recorded(keys,key(X,_),KeyRef),
    erase(KeyRef),
    delete_window(X),
    write($removed window $),
    write(X),nl,
    fail.
```

LISTING 9.9 (Continued next page)

CHAPTER 9 A FEW ARITY PROLOG EXTRAS

```
dw:-
    expunge,
    delete_window(msg),
    delete_window(temp).

dw.

flag_object(Size):-
    tget(R,C),
    NR is R - 1,
    tmove(NR,1),
    Num is Size - 2,
    tchar(Char,Attrib),
    Back is Attrib // 16,
    Forgnd is Attrib mod 16,
    ifthenelse(Forgnd > 8, Foreground is Forgnd - 8, Foreground is Forgnd),
    ifthenelse(Forgnd > 8, Bright is 8, Bright is 0),
    NewAttrib is Foreground * 16 +  Back + Bright,
    wa(Num,NewAttrib),
    tmove(R,C),
    !.

initialize_key(Key):-
    eraseall(Key),
    expunge.

move_object:-
    current_window(Old1,msg),
    cls,
    write($Press RIGHT button to freeze the object position$),
    current_window(_,Old1),
    current(Window),
    recorded(object,windows(Window,TR,TC,BR,BC,T1,T2,T3),Ref),
    abolish(tempsize/4),
    asserta(tempsize(TR,TC,BR,BC)),
    clear_mouse,
    show_mouse_cursor,
    set_mouse_position(TR,TC),
    get_mouse(_,_,-2,_),
    hide_mouse_cursor,
    tempsize(XTR,XTC,XBR,XBC),
    RowChg is XTR - TR,
    ColChg is XTC - TC,
    move_window(RowChg,ColChg),
    replace(Ref,windows(Window,XTR,XTC,XBR,XBC,T1,T2,T3)),
    current_window(Old2,msg),
    cls,
    current_window(_,Old2).
```

LISTING 9.9   (Continued next page)

9.5 AN EXAMPLE

```
name_error:-
    nl,
    write('That name is currently in use, please press return'),
    nl,
    write('and select a different name'),
    read_line(0,_),
    fail.

redraw:-
    key(object,Key),
    nref(Key,First),
    current_window(_,object),
    cls,
    nref(First,Ref),
    redraw_window(Ref).

redraw.

redraw_window(Ref):-
    instance(Ref,windows(X,TR,TC,BR,BC,Title,Attrib1,Attrib2)),
    window_info(Old,_,(_,_),(_,_),(OldAttrib,OldBorder)),
    ChgBorder is abs(OldBorder),
    recolor_window(OldAttrib,ChgBorder),
    ifthenelse(current_window(_,X),current_window(_,X),define_window(X,Title,
            (TR,TC),(BR,BC), (Attrib1,Attrib2))),
    window_info(_,_,(_,_),(_,_),(NewAttrib,NewBorder)),
    ChgNewBorder is -1 * abs(NewBorder),
    recolor_window(NewAttrib,ChgNewBorder),
    relist_attributes(X),
    !,
    nref(Ref,Nref),
    redraw_window(Nref).


resize(_,_,_,4):-
    build_temp(_,_,4),   /* force removal of temp window */
    !.

resize(BR,BC,2,B1):-                    /* resize window */
    tempsize(TR,TC,CBR,CBC),
    RowTest is BR - TR,
    ColTest is BC - TC,
    RowTest > 1,
    ColTest > 1,
    NewRow is BR - CBR,
    NewCol is BC - CBC,
    retract(tempsize(_,_,_,_)),
    asserta(tempsize(TR,TC,BR,BC)),
    resize_window(NewRow,NewCol),
    /* recolor window to erase 'mouse tracks */
```

LISTING 9.9 (Continued next page)

CHAPTER 9 A FEW ARITY PROLOG EXTRAS

```
        window_info(_,_,(_,_),(_,_),(WColor,BColor)),
        recolor_window(WColor,BColor),!.
resize(_,_,2,_):-
        tempsize(_,_,BR,BC),            /* abort this object on negative size */
        set_mouse_position(BR,BC).
resize(NR,NC,-2,B1):-                   /* move window */
        tempsize(TR,TC,CBR,CBC),
        RowChg is NR - TR,
        ColChg is NC - TC,
        BR is CBR + RowChg,
        BR =< 23,
        BC is CBC + ColChg,
        BC =< 78,
        retract(tempsize(_,_,_,_)),
        asserta(tempsize(NR,NC,BR,BC)),
        !.
resize(NR,NC,-2,B1):-                   /* move window */
        tempsize(TR,TC,CBR,CBC),
        RowChg is NR - TR,
        ColChg is NC - TC,
        BR is CBR + RowChg,
        BC is CBC + ColChg,
        (BR > 23 ; BC > 78),
        set_mouse_position(TR,TC),
        !.
resize(_,_,X,_):-
        X =\= 2.
resize_object:-
        current_window(Old1,msg),
        cls,
        write($Press RIGHT button to fix object size$),
        current_window(_,Old1),
        current(Window),
        recorded(object,windows(Window,TR,TC,BR,BC,T1,T2,T3),Ref),
        abolish(tempsize/4),
        asserta(tempsize(TR,TC,BR,BC)),
        set_mouse_position(BR,BC),
        clear_mouse,
        show_mouse_cursor,
        get_mouse(_,_,2,_),
        hide_mouse_cursor,
        tempsize(XTR,XTC,XBR,XBC),
        replace(Ref,windows(Window,XTR,XTC,XBR,XBC,T1,T2,T3)),
        current_window(Old2,msg),
        cls,
        current_window(_,Old2).
```

LISTING 9.9 (Continued)

Index

! (exclamation point), the cut, 31
$$ (double dollar sign), empty string symbol, 52
$ (dollar sign), beginning and ending strings character, 52
% (percent sign), leading comment symbol, 3
* (asterisk), multiplication operator, 19
*/ (asterisk slash), ending comment symbol, 3
+ (plus sign)
  addition operator, 19
  instantiated argument symbol, 77
, (comma), logical and operator, 6, 10
- (minus sign)
  subtraction operator, 19
  uninstantiated argument symbol, 77
. (period)
  end of statement character, 3
  end of term character, 51
/* (slash asterisk), beginning comment symbol, 3
// (double slash), integer division operator, 19
/ (slash), ordinary (real) division operator, 19
:-, if operator (in a rule), 9
; (semicolon)
  key to find the next match, 6
  logical or operator, 6, 11, 67, 71
  Redo command key, 76
<=, less-than-or-equal-to operator (for arithmetic expressions), 20
<
  less-than operator (for arithmetic expressions), 20
  less-than `compare` test symbol, 18
=.., `univ` predicate, 44
=:=, equality operator (for arithmetic expressions), 20
== (double equal sign), "equivalent" operator (for terms), 18
= (equal sign)
  `compare` test symbol, 18
  unification operator, 18
=\=, inequality operator (for arithmetic expressions), 20
>=, greater-than-or-equal-to operator (for arithmetic expressions), 20
>
  greater-than operator (for arithmetic expressions), 20
  greater-than `compare` test symbol, 18
? (question mark), instantiated or uninstantiated argument symbol, 77
@<, less than operator (for terms), 18
@=<, less-than-or-equal-to operator (for terms), 18
@>=, greater-than-or-equal-to operator (for terms), 18
@>, than operator (for terms), 18
[ ] (square brackets)
  the empty list, 35
  list delimiters, 35
\==, not equivalent operator, 18

INDEX

^ (caret), exponential operator, 19
_ (underscore)
  anonymous variable, 6
  multiword name connector, 3
| (vertical bar)
  list head and tail separator, 36, 37
  logical or operator, 6
~ (tilde), accelerator key indicator, 85

`abolish` predicate, 53
Abort command (a key), 76
`abs` function, 20
accelerator key indicator (~), 85
accelerator keys, for activating menus, 85
accept command, ordering Prolog goals, 76
`acos` function, 20
`addhead` predicate, 42
adding clauses to databases, 53–54
addition operator (+), 19
a key, Abort command, 76
ancestor rules, 26–27
anonymous variable (_), 6
append file access mode (a), 58
`append` predicate, 42–44
  query to, illustrated, 43
arguments, 4
  preceded by signs, 77
  referring to rules with an incorrect number of, 71
arithmetic expressions, 19, 20
arithmetic operators, 17, 18–19
arity, 4, 4n
Arity Prolog, ix, 2
  debugging commands in, 76
  menus designing in, 83–87
  mouse information access in, 81
  numbers and math functions in, 21–22
  operators and constants in, 18–20
  special predicates in, 42, 44, 52, 81
  windows designing in, 77–80
  See also PROLOG
arrow keys, for pull-down menus, 87
`asin` function, 20
`asserta` predicate, 53
asserting facts, 62
`assert` predicate, 53
`assertz` predicate, 53
asterisk (*), multiplication operator, 19
asterisk slash (*/), ending comment symbol, 3
a symbol, append file access mode, 58
`atan` function, 20
atoms
  `err`, 21
  `Name`, 84
average temperature celsius rule, 23
average temperature relationship, 22–23

Back to choice point command (x key), 76
backtracking, and the cut, 63–64, 66
b key, Break command, 76
body of a rule, 9
  the cut as, 31
bonus rule, 20
Boolean operators, 6, 10, 11
Break command (b key), 76
`break`, line-drawing menu item, 85
`build_temp` predicate, 90
`build_window` predicate, 90

CALL call, 72
caret (^), exponential operator, 19
carriage return, 32
characters
  for beginning and ending strings ($), 52
  end of term (. + Enter), 51
  reading, 51, 52
  writing, 51, 53
child database, 37

child relationship, 36
circular definitions, 30, 71
circular linked lists for like data storage, 82
c key, Creep command, 72, 76
class relationship, 13
class structures database, 14
clauses, 3, 13
 adding to databases, 53–54
 converting lists to and from, 44–45
 ordering, in the body of a rule, 29, 61–63
 removing from databases, 53, 54
`clear_mouse` predicate, 90
`close` predicate, 57, 58
closing files, 57
`cls` predicate, 47, 55
comma (,)
 logical and operator, 6, 10
 name separator, 3
comments, 3, 67
comment symbols
 beginning (/**), 3
 ending (*/), 3
 leading (%), 3
`compare` operator, 18
comparison operators
 for arithmetic expressions, 20
 for terms, 17, 18
complex rules, 11–12
compound rules, 10–11
conclusions of rules, 9
conditions of rules, 9, 10
 other rules as part of, 11
constants
 name, 3
 real number, 18, 19
`consult` predicate, 53
controlling program execution in PROLOG programs, 61–66
converting lists to clauses and clauses to lists, 44–45
`cos` function, 20
counting elements in lists, 41–42
`create popup` predicate, 79
`create` predicate, 57, 58

creating files, 57
Creep command (c key), 72, 76
`current_window` predicate, 77
cut (!)
 alternatives to, 64, 65
 backtracking and, 63–64, 66
 as the body of a rule, 31
 caution in using, 66
 function of, 63–64
 uses of, 31, 32, 64–65, 66
cut-fail combination, 64–65

database management predicates
 for clauses, 53–54
 for data, 81–83
databases
 adding clauses to, 53–54
 child database, 37
 class structures database, 14
 family database, 5, 27
 liquors database, 22
 location of cities database, 23
 reading and appending clauses from files to, 53–54
 removing clauses from, 53, 54
 stream networks database, 30
 temperatures of cities database, 22–23
 writing clauses to, 53, 54
 See also relationships
debugging commands in Arity Prolog, 72–75, 76
debugging predicates, 72–75
debugging PROLOG programs, 72–76
`define_window` predicate, 77, 78
`delete_window` predicate, 77
designing PROLOG programs, 67, 69–71
dialog box feature, 82
Display goal command (d key), 76
division operators
 integer (//), 19
 ordinary (real) (/), 19
d key, Display goal command, 76

INDEX

documentation, 68, 70
  external, 67
  See also comments
dollar sign ($)
  beginning and end of string character, 52
  using, in a string, 52
double dollar sign ($$), empty string symbol, 52
double equal sign (==), "equivalent" operator (for terms), 18
double slash (//), integer division operator, 19
drains rules, 29, 30
draw menu message, 87

efficiency, improving. *See* writing recursive rule sets
e key, Exit command, 76
elements, of a list, 35
empty list ([]), 35, 39–40
empty string symbol ($$), 52
endless loops, 29–30, 44
end of statement character (.), 3
end of term characters (<.> + <Enter>), 51
Enter key (Creep command), 76
"equality" operator (=:=) (for arithmetic expressions), 20
"equals" symbol (=) (for compare tests), 18
"equivalent" operator (==) (for terms), 18
eraseall predicate, 82, 83
erase predicate, 82, 83
err atom, 21
errors, preventing. *See* writing recursive rule sets
Esc key
  close pull-down menus, 87
  Skip or Quit Help commands, 76
exclamation point (!), the cut, 31
EXIT call, 72
Exit command (e key), 76
exit popup predicate, 79
exp function, 20

exponential operator (^), 19
external documentation, 67

factorial rule, 30–31
  modified to be tail-recursive, 66
  query to (illustrated), 31
facts, 2, 3–4, 10, 16
  ordering, 62
  retracting and asserting, 62
FAIL call, 72
Fail command (f key), 76
fail predicate, 64–65
failure, of goals. *See* goals
family database query menu program, 47–48, 55–56
  suggested enhancements for, 56
family relationship database, 5, 27
file access modes, 58
file I/O predicates, 57–58
  handles of, 57
  as used with standard I/O devices, 57
files
  closing, 57
  creating, 57
  opening, 57
find_it predicate, 55
find_it rules, 54
first predicate, 40
f key, Fail command, 76
floating point operations, 21
float predicate, 21
formatting PROLOG programs, 67
forming lists from information in databases, 54–55
forming new lists, 42–44
functions, math. *See* math functions
get0 predicate, 51, 52
get_mouse_position predicate, 81
get predicate, 51, 52
get_remaining_information predicate, 90
goals, 4, 6. *See also* subgoals

INDEX

go rule, 47, 50, 55, 59
grandmother rule, 10–12
grandparent rules, 26
greater-than operator (>), for arithmetic expressions, 20
greater-than operator (@>), for terms, 18
greater-than-or-equal-to operator (>=), for arithmetic expressions, 20
greater-than-or-equal-to operator (@>=), for terms, 18
greater-than symbol (>), for `compare` tests, 18

handles (H arguments), of file I/O predicates, 57
head of a list, 36
head of a rule, 9
Help command (h key), 76
`hide_mouse_cursor` predicate, 81
`hide_window` predicate, 77
h key, Help command, 76
H symbol
  for the handle of a file I/O predicate, 57
  for the head of a list, 36

if operator (:-) (in a rule), 9, 10
inadvertent recursion, 30, 71
inequality operator (=\=), for arithmetic expressions, 20
infinite loops, 29–30, 44
infix operators, 17
`in` function, 20
`initialize_key` predicate, 87
input and output predicates. *See* I/O predicates
input stream
  reading characters from the current, 51, 52
  reading scan codes from, 52
  reading strings from, 51, 52
  reading terms from the current, 51
`instance` predicate, 82, 83
instantiated argument symbol (+), 77
instantiated or uninstantiated argument symbol (?), 77
instantiation, 6
  of a variable to a clause, 13
instructor rule, 13, 14
`integer` predicate, 21
integers, 21
interpreter prompt, 76
I/O predicates, standard, 51–53
`isalist` predicate, 44
`is_list` predicate, 44
`is` operator, 20, 21

`key` predicate, 82, 83
keys for data storage, 82, 87

last-call optimization. *See* tail-recursion optimization
`last` predicate, 41
Leap command (l key), 75, 76
`length` predicate, 42
less-than operator (<) (for arithmetic expressions), 20
less-than operator (@<) (for terms), 18
less-than-or-equal-to operator (<=) (for arithmetic expressions), 20
less-than-or-equal-to operator (@=<) (for terms), 18
less-than symbol (<) (for `compare` tests), 18
letters
  lower case, 3
  upper case, 5
likes rule, 16
limited world, 2, 61
linked lists, circular, for like data storage, 82
liquors database, 22
list delimiters ([ ]), 35
`list_it` predicate, 55
`list_it` rules, 54
lists, 35–45
  checking for elements of, 38–40
  circular linked lists for like data storage, 82
  converting clauses to and from, 44–45

INDEX

lists (*continued*)
  counting elements in, 41–42
  defined and described, 35
  the empty list ([]), 35, 39–40
  finding elements in particular places in, 40–41
  forming, from information in databases, 54–55
  forming new, 42–44
  printing, 55
  recognizing, 44
  referencing items in, 35–38
  summing elements in, 42
  tables of, 36, 37
  with tails that are not lists, 37–38
l key, Leap command, 75, 76
location of cities database, 23
location relationship, 23
log function, 20
logical and operator (,), 6, 10
logical or operators (;, |), 6, 11, 67, 71
  avoiding the use of, 11, 67, 71
loops, infinite, 29–30, 44
lower case letters, 3

main_loop predicate, 87, 88
main predicate, 87, 88
matching, 4, 4n, 6
math functions, 19, 20, 21–22
member predicate, 38–40
  query to (illustrated), 39
menu clauses, calling other clauses with, 87
menu definition file format, 84
menu definition program, 85
menu(draw) clause, 90
menu drawing program, illustrated, 86
menu items, forms of, 85
menu labels, 85
menu predicate, 87
menus
  designing (in Arity Prolog), 83–87
  removing from the screen, 87
minus sign (-)
  subtraction operator, 19

uninstantiated argument symbol, 77
misspellings, 71
mod (modulo) operator, 19
modular program development, 67, 69–71
mouse, resetting, 90
mouse information access in Arity Prolog, 81
mouse information and positioning program, 82
mouse predicate, 81
mouse predicates, 81
move_window predicate, 77
M symbol, for the head of the tail of a list, 36
multiple rules, 67
multiplication operator (**), 19
multiword name connector (_), 3

name/arity notation for predicates, 4
Name atom, 84
names
  meaningful, 67
  for rules, 13, 67
  for variables, 3
neck of a rule, 9
nested relationships, 13–16
n key, Nodebug command, 76
nl (newline) predicate, 32, 51, 53
Nodebug command (n key), 76
nonrecursive rules, 26–27
north rule, 23
nospy command, removing spy points, 75
nospy predicate, 75
notation for predicates, 4
not equivalent operator (\==), 18
not operator, 18
not predicate, 65
notrace command, quitting the Debugger, 72
notrace predicate, 72
nref predicate, 82, 83
numeric operations, 17–24

INDEX

obj-boxes.art file (of menu definitions), 87
objects, 2
   character or condition of, 3–4
opening files, 57
`open` predicate, 57, 58
   arguments to, 57
operators
   arithmetic, 17, 18–19
   Boolean, 6, 10, 11
   comparison
      for arithmetic expressions, 20
      for terms, 17, 18
   infix, 17, 20
   prefix, 17
   using (examples), 22–24
   See also individual operators by name and symbol
ordering clauses in the body of a rule, 29, 61–63, 70
   importance of, exemplified, 62
ordering facts in a fact set, 62
output stream
   writing characters to, 51, 53
   writing terms to, 51, 52–53

parentheses, to identify ORed items, 6
parent rule, 10, 11, 27
parsing sentences, 52
passing values (in recursion), illustrated, 31, 39, 43
percent rule, 22
percent sign (%), leading comment symbol, 3
period (.)
   end of statement character, 3
   end of term character, 51
`pi` constant, 18, 19
plus sign (+)
   addition operator, 19
   instantiated argument symbol, 77
`p_open` predicate, 57, 58
pop-up windows, 79
predicate name/arity notation, 4
predicates, 4, 18, 19, 21
   arguments to, 4
   arity of, 4
   bonus.lib library of, 81, 81n
   for database management
      of clauses, 53–54
      of data, 81–83
   for debugging, 72–75
   for file I/O, 57–58
   for I/O (standard), 51–53
   for mice, 81
   order of (in the body of a rule), 29–30
   for windows, 78
prefix operators, 17, 18
`pref` predicate, 82, 83
printing lists, 55
`printlist` predicate, 55
`printlist` rule, 55
programs. *See* PROLOG programs
Prolog
   Arity. *See* Arity Prolog
   development of, 1–2
   distinguishing characteristics of, 2, 53
   suitability of, for different tasks, 2
   synonymous terms for, 1
   See also Arity Prolog
PROLOG programs
   controlling program execution in, 61–66
   as databases, 2
   debugging, 72–76
   designing, 67, 69–71
   family database query menu program, 47–48, 55–56
   menu definition program, 85
   menu drawing program, 86
   mouse information and positioning program, 82
   program listing words and punctuation marks in sentences, 49–50, 56–57
   readability of, 67, 71
   reading and displaying text files program, 50, 59
   self-modifying ability of, 45, 53
   types of statements in, 2

PROLOG programs (*continued*)
  window definition program, 88
  windows design programs, 79, 80, 88–96
PROLOG variables, as distinguished from variables in procedural languages, 5n
proof relationship, 22
pull-down menus
  arrow keys for, 87
  definitions of, 85
put predicate, 51, 53

q key, Quasi skip command, 76
Quasi skip command (q key), 76
queries, 4–6, 16
  nested structure of, 38
  semicolons in, 11
  See also databases; lists; query types; questions; relationships; rules; *and individual predicates by name*
query types, 56
  modifying rules for different, 63
  See also queries
question mark (?), instantiated or uninstantiated argument symbol, 77
questions, 2, 4–6. *See also* queries

random constant, 18, 19
ra symbol, read or append file access mode, 58
readability of programs, 67, 71
read or append file access mode (ra), 58
read file access mode (r), 58
reading and appending clauses from files to databases, 53–54
reading characters from the current input stream, 51, 52
reading and displaying text files, program for, 50, 59
reading scan codes from the current input stream, 52

reading strings from the current input stream, 51, 52
reading terms from the current input stream, 51
read_line predicate, 58
read predicate, 51
read_string predicate, 51, 52
read or write file access mode (rw), 58
real numbers, 21
recognizing lists, 44
recolor_window predicate, 77
reconsult predicate, 53
record_after predicate, 82, 83
recorda predicate, 82, 83
recorded predicate, 82, 83
recordz predicate, 82, 83
recursion, 25–33, 38
  defined, 25
  as a generalization of non-recursive rules, 26–29
  inadvertent, 30, 71
  objective of, 25
  passing of values in (illustrated), 31, 39, 43
  stopping conditions in, 27, 29, 32, 41, 64
  tail, 29
recursive rule sets, writing, 29, 44, 55
REDO call, 72
Redo command key (;), 76
reference numbers for data storage, 82
referencing items in lists, 35–38
relabel_window predicate, 77
relationships, 2, 3, 13
  average temperature relationship, 22–23
  child relationship, 36
  class relationship, 13
  family relationship, 5
  location relationship, 23
  nested, 13–16
  proof relationship, 22
  tributary relationship, 29
  See also databases

removing clauses from databases, 53, 54
removing menus from the screen, 87
`repeat` loop, 90
`replace` predicate, 82, 83
report rule, 32
requirements of rules, 9, 10
  other rules as part of, 11
`resetspy` command, removing all spy points, 75
`resetspy` predicate, 75
resetting the mouse, 90
`resize_window` predicate, 77
retracting and asserting facts, 62
`retract` predicate, 53
return values, as single arguments to clauses, 87
room rule, 15–16
`round` predicate, 19
r symbol, read file access mode, 58
rules, 2, 9–12, 16
  ancestor rule, 26–27
  average temperature celsius rule, 23
  bodies of, 9
  bonus rule, 20
  complex, 11–12
  compound, 10–11
  conclusions of, 9
  conditions of, 9, 10
  drains rules, 29, 30
  factorial rule, 30–31
  go rule, 47, 50, 55, 59
  grandmother rule, 10–12
  grandparent rules, 26
  heads of, 9
  instructor rule, 13, 14
  likes rule, 16
  names for, 13, 67
  necks of, 9
  north rule, 23
  parent rule, 10, 11, 27
  parts of, 9
  percent rule, 22
  recursive, 25–32
  report rule, 32
  requirements of, 9, 10

  room rule, 15–16
  semicolons in, 11
  teaches rule, 13, 14
  west rule, 24
  See also clauses; recursion
rule stubs, 71
rw symbol, read or write file access mode, 58

scan codes, reading, 52
scope, of variables, 16
screen, removing menus from, 87
`second` predicate, 40–41
semicolon (;)
  key to find the next match, 6
  logical or operator, 6, 11
  Redo command key, 76
`send_menu_msg` predicate, 86
  general format of, 87
sentences, listing words and punctuation marks in, 49–50, 56–57
`set_mouse_position` predicate, 81
shared variables, 6
`show_mouse_cursor` predicate, 81
`sin` function, 20
s key, Skip command, 76
Skip command (s key), 76
slash (/), ordinary (real) division operator, 19
slash asterisk (/*), beginning comment symbol, 3
`space` key, Toggle between applications and Debugger windows command, 76
spy command, setting spy points, 75
spy points, 75
`spy` predicate, 75
`sqrt` function, 20
square brackets ([ ])
  the empty list, 35
  list delimiters, 35
statements
  general form of, 3
  types of, 2

stopping conditions in recursion, 27, 29, 32, 41, 64
stream networks database, 30
strings, reading, 51, 52
structures, 9, 13–16, 18
   advantages of, 13
   database with, 14, 15
stubs, 71
subgoals, 63. *See also* goals
subtraction operator (-), 19
success, of goals. *See* goals
`sum_list` predicate, 42
summing elements in lists, 42
syntax
   for arithmetic expressions, 19
   for facts, 3
   for infix operators, 17, 20
   for integers, 21
   for lists, 35, 36
   for math functions, 21–22
   for predicates, 4, 17, 38
   for rules, 9
   for structures, 13
syntax errors, 71

`tab` predicate, 51, 53
tail of a list, 36, 37
tail recursion, 29, 63
tail-recursion optimization, 63–65
`tan` function, 20
teaches rule, 13, 14
temperatures of cities database, 22–23
terms
   reading, 51
   writing, 51, 52–53
text files, reading and displaying, 50, 59
the cut. *See* cut (!)
tilde (~), 85
`tmove` predicate, 81
Toggle between applications and Debugger windows command (`space` key), 76
top-down programming, 67
towers of Hanoi puzzle, 25–26, 32–33
   algorithm for, 25, 33
   illustrated, 26
   program solution for, 32
trace calls, 72
trace command, starting the Debugger, 72
trace examples, 72–73, 72–75
`trace` predicate, 72
trace prompt, 72
tributary relationship, 29
T symbol, for the tail of a list, 36

unbound variables, 66
underscore (_)
   anonymous variable, 6
   multiword name connector, 3
unification, 4, 4n
unification operator (=), 18, 21
uninstantiated argument symbol (-), 77
`univ` predicate (=..), 44
upper case letters, 5

values, passing (in recursion), illustrated, 31, 39, 43
variables
   anonymous, 6
   as instantiated to clauses, 13
   names for, 3
   as place holders, 5
   scope of, 16
   shared, 6
   unbound, 66
   unlike procedural language variables, 5n
   as used for stating facts, 8
vertical bar (|)
   list head and tail separator, 36, 37
   logical or operator, 6

west rule, 24
`what_windows` predicate, 77
"who" questions, 6
`window_info` predicate, 77
windows
   building new, 90–92
   designing (in Arity Prolog), 77–80
   manipulating, 92–96

windows design programs
  elaborate, 88–96
  simple, 79, 80
windows predicates, 78
w key, Write goal command, 76
write file access mode (w), 58
Write goal command (w key), 76
`write` predicate, 32, 51, 52
`writeq` predicate, 51, 53
writing characters to the current output stream, 51, 53
writing clauses to databases, 53, 54
writing recursive rule sets, 29–30, 44
writing terms to the current output stream, 51, 52–53
w symbol, write file access mode, 58

x key, Back to choice point command, 76

Zip command (z key), 76
z key, Zip command, 76